The

Collector

and other tales…

Callie Hill

www.literaturelove.co.uk

THE STORY COLLECTOR

First published in Great Britain in 2021 by
Literature Love Ltd
Bristol, United Kingdom.

A CIP catalogue record for this book is available
from the British Library.

Hardback ISBN 978-1-914212-01-7
Paperback ISBN 978-1-914212-00-0
e-book ISBN 978-1-914212-02-4

Cover design by Callie Hill and Louis Hill.
Images courtesy of Adobe Stock.

To my mum and dad, Grace and Albert Long – the best parents any child could ever wish for. For Mum, who showed me that a cuddle and a good book could solve almost any problem; and for Dad, who taught me you can also make up your own stories. One day, I will bring Harold the Mouse to life in print, just for you, Dad!

xxx

THE STORY COLLECTOR

We are what we repeatedly do.
Excellence, therefore, is not an act
but a habit

Aristotle (384 – 322BC)

Or possibly not Aristotle – who cares?
It's still my favourite quote…

THE STORY COLLECTOR

Contents

THE STORY COLLECTOR

Colin

The Story Collector – Part 1

The last two weeks had seen an Indian summer and the popular suntrap of Bristol's College Green was awash with office workers and students making the most of their lunch break. *A perfect day for people watching* Colin thought as he waited in the queue at the sandwich bar that overlooked the green. He tapped the inside pocket of his cream blazer, double-checking he'd remembered to bring his writing journal and favourite pen that his wife had bought for his sixtieth birthday. Tomorrow night he was meeting with his writing group. Each month, a different member of the group would host the meeting at their home, and a couple of other members would read out what they'd been working on. This month, the meeting was being held at Paula's house. Colin was on the list to read out his

1

work, but was suffering from writer's block and couldn't think of anything to write about. His last piece of fiction had been a joy to write, and the feedback he'd received from his writing group had been crucial in honing his story. He was so pleased with it he'd decided to self-publish and the proof copies had arrived in the post that morning. It would be a challenge to write something of the same calibre for his next project, but he'd caught the self-publishing bug and was determined to do the same for his next story. Hopefully, the fresh air and sunshine would give him some inspiration.

'Sorry, mate, didn't see you there.' It was one of the young men standing in front of him in the queue. The pair were talking loudly and the shorter one with dark hair had stepped backwards into Colin, forcing him to topple. But the young man's nonchalant tone as he apologised, suggested he wasn't sorry at all. Had it not been for Colin's walking stick and the help of the woman standing behind him, he would have fallen over.

'Well, perhaps you should pay more attention to what's going on around you instead of what's on your phone.' The woman behind Colin interrupted. 'This poor gentleman almost fell over.'

'What's it got to do with you?' He raised his arm

and waved his phone in the air, almost hitting the woman in the face with it.

'There's no need for that,' Colin said. 'Show some respect.' It wasn't just the way the young man had spoken to the woman that had upset Colin, but the picture that he'd noticed on his phone.

'Alright, Grandad. Keep your hair on. If you've got any under that hat, that is.' He flicked the brim of Colin's straw boater, laughing as he did so.

But Colin didn't retaliate. He would get his revenge through other means. People really shouldn't mess with a writer…

to be continued…

Abby

Literature, Latte, and Love

Abby was spoiled for choice whether to spend her lunch break strolling along Bristol's harbourside, browsing the array of indie shops on Park Street, or just relaxing in the glorious sunshine on College Green. Choosing the latter, she found an ideal spot under a tree, and lay her jacket on the grass, before sitting down to eat her lunch. She'd just opened her lunchbox when her phone pinged. As she looked at the notification, everything around her seemed to slow down; thrum of the nearby city centre fading away as the only sound she could hear was the drumming of her own heartbeat. It was a simple decision to most. Swipe right or swipe left. Yes or no. But having gone through more heartache than most women twice her age, Abby wasn't used to making such a big decision. However, since her thirtieth birthday two weeks ago, she was determined to make a fresh start. She'd finally faced the fact that Lee wasn't coming back. Ever. And tapping on the notification, she swiped right before she changed her mind.

Reassured that she'd taken the first step in coming to terms with the past and accepting whatever the future held, Abby took a bite of her sandwich, laying back against the tree as she settled into reading *The Duchess of Malfi* - the play she was currently studying for her literature degree with the Open University. The poor widowed duchess was currently locked in a dungeon, facing death at the hands of her evil brothers for daring to fall in love with a man of her own choice and Abby was at that point in the story where she didn't want to put the book down.

The sun filtered through the tree, kissing Abby's bare legs as she lost herself in the story of the young widow. But as much as she would have rather stayed exactly where she was all afternoon, striking of the cathedral clock told her it was a quarter to the hour, which meant it was, unfortunately, time to return to the office. Not only that, she'd spotted a portly middle-aged man, wearing a cream blazer and straw boater hat, hobbling across the green towards her with his walking stick. Colin, her boss.

'Beautiful day.' Colin said, as he stopped to rest.

'It certainly is.'

'Just the weather for a good book. See you back at the office.' Colin tipped the brim of his hat towards her before walking through to the other side of the green.

Abby watched Colin as he hobbled away. The scorching midday sun had persuaded everybody else to ditch their jackets, either using them as a picnic blanket or scrunching them behind their neck as a make-shift pillow; but with Colin still wearing his trademark cream blazer, it made him stand out from the crowd. He seemed a serious sort of person to Abby, but she'd heard that Colin had sprained his ankle playing Frisbee with his dog. He also belonged to a writers' group and had a reputation for writing stories that were so magical, it was as if his characters were real people.

The next day, Abby woke up to Oscar, her golden spaniel, licking her face. Since Lee had been killed in action in Afghanistan, three years ago, Oscar sensed his absence; preferring Lee's side of the bed to his basket downstairs in the kitchen.

'Good morning, boy.' She kissed Oscar on the top of his head. 'And good morning to you too, babes.' Abby reached over and kissed the photograph of Lee, handsome in his uniform on their wedding day. People often told her time was a healer, but it felt every time she took a step forward then something else sent her spiralling backwards. She was used to Lee being away from home for long periods at a time, but knowing he wasn't ever coming home made the house seem emptier somehow. Oscar wasn't much more than a puppy when Lee was killed. It had taken time, but gradually Abby accepted that Lee was gone forever, and Oscar filled the void that Lee had left behind. But no sooner had the place seemed like home again, with just her and Oscar, the landlord's new wife decided that when the lease on Abby's two-up, two-down, terraced house expired, pets would no longer be permitted. The clock was ticking and finding a place for them both to live was becoming an impossible task.

After a quick shower and breakfast, Abby collected up Oscar's things and walked next door to Mary's house. Mary had also lost her husband, albeit under different circumstances, and offered to dog-sit for Oscar whilst Abby was at work. In return, Abby fetched any bits and pieces that Mary needed from the supermarket and put her bins and recycling out on collection day. Although Mary was over seventy years of age, her granddaughter, Jemma, made sure she was up to speed with all the latest technology, and it had been Mary who'd convinced Abby into setting up a Tinder account.

'I know you think you'll never meet anybody who'll match up to Lee. Maybe you won't. Maybe you don't want to,' Mary had told her. 'But you'll never know unless you try. Lee would hate to think of you being so miserable all the time, my love. But that's not going to change unless you do something about it.'

It was the bit that Mary had said about her not wanting to meet anybody who might make her as happy as Lee did, that hit home. Lee would never be able to do all the things they'd planned to do together, so why should she? Was she subconsciously punishing herself? Or was it the thought of achieving all her hopes and dreams, with somebody other than Lee by her side, that scared her? Either way, Mary was right, Lee wouldn't want her to sit back whilst her life gradually faded away. And now, after swiping right yesterday, she was going on a date with Blake at *The Lush Vine*, the wine bar near the office.

'Good morning, my love,' Mary said as she answered the door. 'And you too, Oscar.'

Abby barely had a chance to unclip Oscar's lead before he shot past Mary, through the hallway and into the kitchen, where Mary had a bowl of milk waiting for him. She often wondered whether Oscar had been a cat in a previous life.

'Now, don't you go rushing back tonight. Oscar's never any trouble. I don't mind him staying here as long as you need.'

'Thank you, Mary.' Abby reached out and touched the older woman's arm. 'I'm going to miss you so much when I move.'

'The feeling's mutual, my love. How's your house-hunting going?'

'Not good. Everything is either out of my price range, or they don't allow dogs. But there's no way I can give up Oscar.'

'Well, like I've already told you, you know you're welcome to stay with me until you find something suitable.'

'You've been so kind to me, Mary. I don't know how I would've got through the last couple of years without you.'

'Oh, get away with you, you'll make me blush. Just make sure you forget all your troubles for tonight and enjoy yourself. You deserve a bit of happiness after everything you've been through. Now, where's that picture of this young man, you said you were going to show me?'

Abby took her phone out of her bag and showed Mary the picture of Blake, her date for the evening.

'This is him. Handsome, isn't he?'

'Hmm, yes.' Mary returned the phone, the smile slipping from her face. 'You go careful, my love. And don't feel pressurised into going out on a date just because of what I said. I'm too interfering for my own good sometimes. You're still young. You have all the time in the world to find somebody who will love you the way your Lee did.'

'I will. Be careful that is. And no, you haven't pressured me into anything. You're right, I do need to take control of my life.' It wasn't strictly true, not at first. Abby felt meeting somebody else was something she needed to do to help her move on, rather than something she wanted; but now she was looking forward to a night out for a change.

At work, the morning was mostly taken up with the weekly team meeting. There seemed something different about Colin; he'd dragged his heels over just about everything, delegating tasks to Abby that weren't in her job description, making it clear that she needed to action everything before she left the office that evening. Any other time she would have commented on the excessive workload, but tomorrow was her big interview. The company was expanding, and Colin needed an assistant manager. She'd been his PA for several years, but there was stiff competition for the role. This would prove she could deal with whatever tasks were thrown at her. And the pay rise that came with the assistant manager's position would mean being able to afford a suitable place for her and Oscar.

It was now half past three. With an hour and a half to go before the end of her working day, the only urgent thing on her 'to-do' list was to type up the report that Colin had sent to Winscribe, her digital dictation e-box. Her hard work had paid off, and as much as she was annoyed with Colin for dumping so much work on her, she now felt a sense of achievement. As Abby put on her headset to type the report, she noticed a text message flash up on her phone.

Can't wait to meet you later.

Can't wait to meet you too ☺ Abby wondered whether to finish the text with an 'x' or not, before deciding to use a smiley face emoji instead. Friendly but not too keen.

Need to meet a bit earlier. Is 5 on the dot ok?

I don't finish work til 5 ☹ she texted back.

Can you get away early? Looking 4ward 2 r

date.

OK ☺

As she pressed 'send' she realised bringing things forward by half an hour would be cutting things fine if she was going to freshen up and change into her new pale-blue skater dress, before going on her date, but it was too late to change her reply now. Blake would think she was ditsy and indecisive. Not the impression she wanted to make at all. She'd just have to ask Colin if she could leave early and finish typing the report in the morning. But first she needed to get into his good books.

Taking the packet of two individually wrapped jammy dodger biscuits out of her desk drawer, Abby made her way to the kitchen – an area just off the main open-plan office. Justin, who worked in accounts, was sitting at the small round table. Most of her colleagues took their drinks back to their desk, but Justin only made coffee at set times of the day and would sit in the kitchen whilst he drank it.

'Hello Justin,' Abby said. 'Are you ready for the interview tomorrow?' Abby flicked on the kettle, took two mugs out of the cupboard, adding a spoonful of coffee to each, and a spoonful of sugar to Colin's mug.

'Of course,' Justin said. 'I've been revising the

company's core values and with all my experience, I'm pretty sure I'll be offered the post. Although, I shouldn't be telling you that. With you being the enemy.'

'I think you mean competitor, not enemy, Justin.' Abby walked over to the table and pulled out one of the plastic chairs, sitting down whilst she waited for the kettle to boil.

'If you say so.' With his legs crossed, Justin bounced his top leg up and down, his arms folded across his chest.

'Well, good luck, anyway. I mean it, Justin. Obviously, I want the job. But if you get it, then I would have lost to a strong candidate.' The kettle boiled and she stood up, returning to the mugs of coffee and pouring boiling water over them.

'I thought Colin took sugar in his coffee?' Justin said.

'He does,' Abby said. 'His has sugar in.'

'I didn't see you add any. You should put some brown sugar in. Colin likes that. It's healthier than white sugar. A bit like brown bread is healthier than white bread.'

'Is it?' Abby had no idea whether or not it was true, and she was pretty sure she'd already added sugar. But an extra spoonful might help sweeten

Colin up.

'Yes. Trust me. Colin will love it.' Justin walked over to one of the cupboards and opened the door. I'm sure it's in here somewhere.'

'It's on the top shelf,' Abby said.

'I can't see it anywhere.'

'Let me look.'

Justin stood back to let Abby reach for the sugar. His plan had worked and whilst she wasn't looking, he took the salt cellar that had previously been on the table, but was now in his pocket, and added a generous dose of salt to Colin's mug.

As Abby carried the two cups of coffee back to her work area, she walked past the open-plan section of the accounts department. Stella, one of the account managers, always took time to speak to Abby, and after such a hectic day, it made a pleasant respite to stop and speak to her colleague.

'Somebody's being spoilt.' Stella said. 'I hope Colin appreciates it.'

'I hope so too,' Abby told her. 'I need to leave early, so I've added an extra spoonful of sugar, to sweeten him up.'

'Good plan,' Stella said. 'He seemed to have something on his mind when I spoke to him earlier.'

'You noticed too? I don't know what's got into him, he's not usually this much of a nightmare to work for.'

'No, he's not, is he. I've known him for years before I came to work here. It's odd that he's acting so strange.'

'Let's hope he's okay, and just having an off day,' Abby said as she walked away, wishing her hands were free so she could cross her fingers. She didn't want him to be in this mood for her interview tomorrow.

'There you go, Colin.' Abby placed the mug of coffee on Colin's desk, together with the jammy dodgers.

'Thanks,' he said, bringing the mug to his lips and savouring the aroma. 'Have you finished typing that report yet?'

Jeez, what kind of superpower does he think I have? It had only arrived in her dictation e-box an hour ago. 'Almost done,' she lied. 'Actually Colin,' Abby tucked her hair behind her ear before biting her lip, 'I was just wondering if it would be okay if...'

Colin was about to take a sip of his coffee when his phone rang. He placed his mug down before taking the call, cutting Abby off mid-sentence.

'Hi. I'll be in lat... Yes, I remember... Go

ahead… Really? Small world… Not at all. Quite appropriate in the circumstances… Yes… Yes, I see… Hm… Sounds like a plan… Just one moment.' Colin placed the receiver close to his chest before turning to Abby. 'If that's all, Abby? I need to take this call.'

Abby walked back to her desk, wishing she hadn't bothered with the extra spoonful of sugar. And definitely not the biscuits. The digital clock on her computer showed it was 3:49. She needed to leave by half past four if she was going to get changed before heading over to *The Lush Vine* to meet Blake at five o'clock, but going by the mood Colin was in, she wouldn't be getting away from the office early tonight. She'd just have to text Blake and tell him she couldn't make it. It would have to be an early night with her PJs and a book instead. The only romance Abby was going to get was by transporting herself into the world of the heroines in the novels she read.

Abby thought about her current heroine. The duchess had believed everybody she loved was dead and wanted to die herself; but when she realised it was all a lie, it was too late. But whilst it was too late for The Duchess of Malfi to stand up for herself, it wasn't too late for Abby. Her story might be a tragic one, but unlike the duchess, she was determined it wouldn't end that way. She'd done everything Colin had asked of her today. That would go in her favour at the interview tomorrow. And now it was time to show how assertive she could be.

Abby stood up to walk over to Colin's desk when she noticed he was limping over to her. 'Colin, I was just coming to see you.'

'Sorry Abby, it's going to have to wait. I have to dash off – well not dash exactly.' Colin looked down towards his bandaged ankle. It was the first time Abby had seen him smile all day. 'I have a hospital appointment, but I'm afraid I've double-booked myself. I was wondering, if you left here a little early, whether you could fetch my blazer from the dry cleaners. I will need it to wear at the interviews tomorrow.'

Abby realised that's what was different about him. With him being more stressed than usual and dumping more work onto her, she'd missed the fact that his jacket wasn't hanging from the back of his chair during the meeting. It was like he was a different person without it.

'Sorry, I know it's on the other side of town, but you live over that way, don't you? If you left a few minutes early, it shouldn't be too much out of your way. I'd be really grateful.'

17

'I do, but I'm supposed to be meet…'

'Oh, and by the way, can you pop these books into the café just over the road from the dry cleaners?' He handed her a pile of books. The one on the top of the pile was John Webster's *The Duchess of Malfi.*

'I didn't realise you'd read this?' Abby said. 'I'm reading it at the moment.'

'Yes. It's a very sad story, isn't it?' he said.

'Terribly sad,' Abby agreed. 'It's a shame she didn't stand up to her awful brothers sooner.'

She looked through the pile. There was *Persuasion* by Jane Austen*; Gone With the Wind* by Margaret Mitchell; a book on fairy tales with a picture of Cinderella on the front cover; and at the bottom of the pile was a book that Abby had never heard of: *Literature, Latte, and Love* by Amy Nicholl. The book looked as if it had come straight off the press, the spine completely intact.

'I wouldn't have thought this was your kind of thing?'

'Oh, there's probably quite a lot you don't know about me,' Colin said, wagging his finger. 'All the best literature has an element of romance. Now, don't forget to drop the books off, will you? It's a great little place, lets you borrow books for free. All you have to do is tell the owner a story of your own. See you tomorrow.' Colin turned and walked out of the office, waving his hand in the air.

Checking the time on her Fitbit watch, Abby saw it was 3:57. The dry cleaners was a twenty-minute journey each way. She was lucky enough to have an allocated car space in the company's underground car park. If she left the office now, it would cut things fine to get back into the city in time to meet Blake at 5 o'clock, but it was doable. She didn't want to face her interview with Colin in a foul mood because he didn't have his cream blazer. She would just have to take the risk and hope the rush-hour traffic was on her side.

***

Abby turned up the radio in her red Corsa. *Things Can Only Get Better,* Howard Jones sang to her, and she believed him. Despite the overcast, steel-grey sky, she had a good feeling about tonight. September had always been her favourite month; even more so since she'd become a mature student - that back to school, fresh new start feeling. As much as she'd have given anything to change the past and still have

Lee in her life, that was impossible and it was time she faced up to her future.

As usual, the high street was busy and Abby had no choice but to park on one of the side streets. She stepped out of the car, taking her tote bag full of Colin's books from the passenger seat. She grabbed her jacket, then put it back down again. Her bag was heavy enough as it was, and it was far too hot to wear it.

She made her way to the dry cleaners and an old-fashioned bell pinged as she pushed open the door.

'Hello Abby.' Jemma, Mary's granddaughter, stepped down from a stool and raised her hands to her chest. 'Fancy seeing you here.'

'Hello, Jemma. I didn't mean to startle you. I've just come for my boss's cream blazer. The same one that I brought in a couple of months ago.'

'Yes, I know the one,' she said. 'How's Oscar? He's such a sweetie. Grandma loves having him.'

'Aw, I know. Oscar loves staying with Mary, too. Look, I don't mean to sound rude, but I don't have time to talk just now. I'm in a rush.' Abby handed Jemma the ticket. 'It should be ready to pick up.'

'Yes,' Jemma said. 'Wait here. I'll just fetch it.' She moved the stool away from the doorway behind the counter.

'But isn't it here...?' Abby pointed to the rail of clothing just to the left of the serving counter. There was a sign above the rail saying 'For Collection' and the items were all covered in plastic dust jackets. But Jemma had already disappeared through the doorway that led to the storeroom at the back of the shop.

Abby looked up at the digital clock above the door. It was 4:15. Despite the traffic, it hadn't taken her as long to get here as she'd expected. She walked over to the shop-front window. From here she had a good view of the high street. The coffee shop that Colin had instructed her to deliver the books to was directly opposite, on the corner of the side street where she'd parked her car. She saw it was called *The Story Collector* and remembered how Colin had told her the owner let customers borrow books in return for a story of their own. One window was taken up with a display of books, and through the other Abby could see people sitting drinking cups of tea or coffee. *I wonder who owns such a place*, she thought.

Jemma seemed to be taking forever. *What an earth could she be up to?* Abby pressed the brass bell on the desk and Jemma came back into the shop.

'Sorry, Abby. Um, where were we?'

'You're supposed to be fetching my boss's blazer. As I said, I'm in rather a hurry.'

'Oh yes. I'm so sorry. I won't be two ticks.'

Abby took a deep breath and blew out slowly. The clock told her it was now 4:35. Had it been anybody else serving she would have been kicking up a fuss by now, but with Jemma being Mary's granddaughter, it didn't seem right to have a go at her. Instead, she tapped her fingers on the counter extra loudly. *I should have dropped the books in whilst I was waiting,* she thought.

A few more minutes and Jemma reappeared. 'It's okay, panic over. My colleague put it on this rail.' She walked over to the 'For Collection' rail.

Abby's phone pinged. A text from Blake: *C U soon x.*

Won't be long. Running a bit late ☹ she texted back.

Abby contemplated leaving dropping off the books for another time. She didn't want to keep Blake waiting but realised that keeping Colin sweet, and by extension the chance of promotion and being able to afford a place to live, was a higher priority. She would have to forget about changing into her new dress. After all, it was Blake's idea to meet straight from work.

The earlier steel-grey sky had turned to deep-slate, and it had started to drizzle with rain. Abby cursed herself for not bringing her jacket with her as she ran across the road to the café. As soon as she stepped inside, she was hit with the aroma of freshly ground coffee mingled with old books. There was a floor to ceiling bookshelf along the back wall, and a Labrador lay next to a woman's feet as she sat reading in a big squishy armchair.

'Hello there. I won't be a sec.' The barista was busy serving, and there was a queue three customers deep, but he still took the time to welcome Abby.

'No worries,' Abby said, as an idea came to her. 'Is it okay if I use your loo?' She'd learned her lesson, hanging about waiting at the dry cleaners. It was time to do some multi-tasking.

The toilet at the back of the shop was much bigger than Abby had expected. Not only was there some gorgeous smelling handwash but also a matching dispenser of hand cream. There was also a full-length mirror. After a quick freshen up of her make-up, Abby changed into her dress. She'd had every intention of hanging the dress up in her locker at work, but with one thing and another it had completely slipped her mind. Although it had been at the bottom of her tote bag all day, luckily it wasn't creased at all, and the cut of the dress suited her. Looking in the full-length mirror, she was glad she'd taken the time to change out of her work clothes.

'Hello again. You didn't have to change just for me, you know,' the barista said, simultaneously giving a wolf whistle.

The barista's whistle sounded exactly like the way Lee used to whistle at her when she'd dressed up for a night out with him, and for a moment it stunned her into not being able to speak or move.

'Um, no it's because I um, well I have to go somewhere.' Abby fumbled in her bag.

'I'm only kidding,' he said. His eyes crinkled up at the corners when he spoke. 'What can I get you?'

'Oh, I'm not here to buy anything. I just came to give you these.' Abby reached into her bag, pulled out the books, and placed them on the counter.

'Thanks. Are you sure I can't tempt you? I can personally recommend the blueberry muffins, fresh out of the oven, I made them myself.'

Abby's phone pinged again. *Where R U?*

'Sorry. I'm running late as it is.' She walked over and opened the door leading back out onto the high street. Big fat raindrops were falling fast, and she hesitated. Her dress would be ruined; not to mention Colin's dry cleaning.

'I could lend you this if you like, Abby?' The barista held out a bright red golfing umbrella.

Puzzled, Abby turned and looked at him. 'Did you just call me Abby?'

'You are Abby, aren't you? Please tell me I haven't just made a complete idiot of myself.'

'Yes, I am. But how did you know?' Abby walked back over to the counter.

'Uncle Colin said somebody called Abby was bringing his research books back at the same time as collecting his dry cleaning. And going by what's draped over your arm, I guess that must be you. I'm Lucas, by the way.' He handed her the umbrella.

'Did you say *Uncle* Colin?' A fizz of electricity shot through her as they brushed hands when she took the umbrella from him.

'Yeah. He's my mum's brother. He owns this place, so he's my boss too. See, we have something in common already.' Lucas picked the books up from the counter and looked through the pile. He held up the book called *Literature, Latte, and Love* by Amy Nicholl. 'Ah, he's such a romantic.'

'I still can't believe he would read that sort of thing,' Abby said.

'Read it. He writes it! Amy Nicholl is Uncle Colin's pseudonym. It's an anagram for Colin

Hamly.'

'Really? And did you say the other books were for research?'

'Yes. Although he does his proper research by what he calls people watching. He likes to think that by turning people he's met into a character in one of his books, he can change their lives.'

'Wow, he really is a romantic.'

'Oh, not always. He writes thrillers too. Some of his characters come to a very grisly end. Uncle Colin has a very vivid imagination; I have no idea where he gets it from. It's been fun having him stay here. Although I wonder what he has in store for some tales our customers have told him.'

'He's staying here?'

'Yes. Him and Auntie Pat are staying in the empty flat upstairs. They've got the builders in at home at the moment. I live in the flat at the front, and Uncle Colin is staying in the one at the back. Billie here is his dog.' Lucas nodded towards the Labrador sitting next to the woman in the armchair. 'I'm going to miss the company when they've gone. Especially Billie. But don't tell her that.'

'So, if he's staying here, why has he asked me to collect his dry cleaning and drop off these books?' Billie wandered over to Abby and she reached down and ruffled her ears.

'Oh, he's a mind unto his own is Uncle Colin. If I didn't know any better... oh wait...' Lucas turned over *Literature, Latte, and Love,* and read the blurb printed on the back. He laughed out loud at Colin's choice of Babs and Claus for the character names.

Abby's phone pinged. A text from Blake. *Soz babe can't wait any longer.*

'You okay? You've gone a bit pale.' Lucas walked around to the other side of the counter and led Abby to one of the squishy sofas.

She felt a pang of guilt as she thought of Blake waiting for her, but the abruptness of his text quashed this. Somehow, he didn't seem to matter now.

'It's nothing important,' she told Lucas. 'Do you know what? I think I might try one of your blueberry muffins after all.'

'Of course, madam. Coming straight up. Going by the blurb on the back of "her" book, Amy Nicholl will be pleased.'

***

Colin watched with satisfaction as the young men that he'd been observing walked out of *The Lush*

Vine. It had been a productive 'people watching' exercise where he'd made detailed notes on the idiosyncrasies of his next characters. The way the short, dark-haired one kept checking his phone, tapping away at the screen as it became apparent that his date wasn't going to turn up. The smug sense of satisfaction as the taller, rangy one realised he would win the bet. As Colin was putting his notebook into his bag, his phone rang.

'Alright, Colin. How's it going? Did I stall her long enough?'asked Jemma.

'Yes, you did great. The look on his face once he realised she wasn't coming was a picture. Talking of which, I took one, so I'll send it to you.'

'What a loser. Abby had a close escape. Oh, and I put the clock back ten minutes as well. That threw her. She had no idea how late she was.'

'You're good at this,' Colin laughed. 'So is your grandmother.'

Colin was glad that both Abby and Jemma were no longer involved with the idiot he'd seen yesterday at lunchtime. It was just before he'd seen Abby on College Green. The queue in the sandwich bar had snaked right out of the door onto Park Street. Nothing unusual, as the place was popular at lunchtimes. Most customers were standing patiently waiting their turn, but the two young men in front of him were talking loudly and waving a phone in the air.

'No way, she won't fall for it. She's way above your league mate,' the rangy one with fair hair said.

'Bet she would.' The shorter, dark-haired guy seemed sure of himself.

'Okay. Put your money where your mouth is. Usual twenty quid says she won't wait more than fifteen minutes.'

'You're on,' Shorty said, stumbling backwards and almost knocking Colin over.

A young woman in the queue stuck up for him; told the man to be more careful. But he argued with her, and as he did so Colin took a double-take as he noticed the picture of Abby on the screen of the man's phone. He had no idea what Shorty and his accomplice were up to at that point, but had a feeling that whatever it was they were trying to set Abby up. On his way back to the office, he'd stopped and spoken to her as she was sitting reading on the grass under the tree. She looked happier than she had in ages. He had to stop those pair of clowns from causing her more pain – but how?

When he arrived back at his flat that evening, Colin was sitting downstairs in the café. He'd always thought Abby and Lucas would make a great couple, with their joint passion for literature and latte, and six months ago had decided to bring them together through the characters of Babs and Claus. It wasn't always possible to find anagrams of the real-life version of his characters, but Babs was only one letter away from Abby, and Claus contained all the same letters as Lucas. He found the closer he was to a match in name, the more likely his stories were to come true. With Abby having lost her husband in such tragic circumstances, and not knowing whether she was ready to move on just yet, he'd felt it inappropriate to match-make before now; but after the incident he'd witnessed at lunchtime, this changed things. All he needed to do was to get Abby and Lucas to meet in real life, as well as in his story.

As usual, Billie was in high spirits to see him.

'Steady on, girl,' Colin said.

But it was too late. Billie had already jumped up, spilling coffee all over Colin's cream blazer.

The dry cleaners was only just over the road, so he went over straight away before they closed for the evening. As soon as he handed over his jacket, he noticed the assistant had been crying.

'You okay?' he asked.

'Nothing a hit man couldn't solve,' she said, as she rubbed her eyes with the back of her hand. 'Just found out my boyfriend has been perving after other girls on Tinder. He has this thing going with Rik – that's his mate - where they see who can get the most dates, then they film the girl waiting for them to see how long it is before she gives up and leaves.'

'Sounds like a right charmer.'

'That's the thing with online profiles. He looks like Mr Nice Guy if you don't know him. Look.' Jemma showed Colin her boyfriend's profile. 'They've always competed with each other. At school it was sport, then who had the best car, but lately it's been women.'

'Well, it sounds like you're much better off without him.'

Colin recognised the guy in the picture as the same person he'd seen in the sandwich bar. Abby deserved to know, but how could he say anything without coming across as being a stalker, knowing the ins and outs of her personal life? The only thing he could do was try to delay her at work so she'd be late for her date.

It had surprised him when Jemma had called that afternoon.

'Hi, this is Jemma from the dry cleaners. Is that Colin?'

'Yes, it is. Hi, I'll be in lat...'

'Do you remember me telling you about my loser of a boyfriend when you came in with your blazer?'

'Yes, I remember.'

'Well, I've got a huge favour to ask.'

'Go ahead.' Colin was intrigued. If it meant he could play a small part in bringing down the low life who thought he could mess around with the emotions of a grieving war widow, then he was all ears.

'You probably don't know this, but your secretary, Abby, well she lives next door to my gran.'

'Really? Small world.'

'And that dickhead of a boyfriend of mine, sorry excuse my French...'

'Not at all. Quite appropriate in the circumstances.'

'Well, according to my gran, he's meeting Abby tonight. Or so she thinks.'

'Yes....' This was something he knew.

'But we have to stop her from turning up. We need to turn the tables on him. He always meets his date in *The Lush Vine* by the bar. There's a small area over the far side that's hidden away behind a pillar, but has a good view of whoever comes in. That's where he and Rik will be hiding.'

'Yes, I see.'

'What I was thinking was, if you could get Abby to fetch your dry cleaning for you, and like don't tell her until the last minute. She lives over this way so you could tell her to fetch it on her way home or something.'

'Hmm…'

'And I could stall her here, then she'd be late and he'd think he'd been stood up.'

'Sounds like a plan.'

Colin looked at the pile of books on his desk. His author copy of *Literature, Latte, and Love* had arrived in the post before he'd left for work that morning. In his story Babs was the one who worked in a coffee shop, Claus was a customer who'd walked straight into her when she was carrying a tray of drinks. It wasn't quite the same story, but Jemma's plan to delay Abby by getting her to fetch the dry cleaning had given him an idea. He just needed an excuse to get Abby into the coffee shop – and his pile of books could be the perfect answer.

'Just one thing,' Colin said to Jemma as he walked out of *The Lush Vine.* 'Did you see if Abby went into the café?' He needed to know if the final touches to his plan had worked.

33

'Yes, she did. What makes you ask? Did you tell her about the flat?'

'The flat?'

'She's been finding it difficult to find somewhere for her and Oscar, her dog.'

'Oh? I didn't realise she was moving.'

'Yes, her landlord's new wife says she doesn't like dogs. But Gran thinks it's just an excuse to split the house into bedsits and make more money.'

'Poor Abby, having to deal with that on her own. Thanks for letting me know. I feel quite terrible for the pressure I've put her under at work today.'

Before today, Colin had Justin, who worked in accounts, down as the strongest candidate for the assistant manager's post, but after the way Abby had dealt with everything thrown at her, he realised she was the best person for the job. She'd even made him a coffee. He felt guilty about letting it go cold and having to throw it away, but he still appreciated the thought on her part. She'd make a great tenant for the flat, too. Things looked like they might work out even better than Colin had anticipated. *It's true what they say,* he thought. *Real life really is more interesting than fiction.* And now he had an idea for another story. Not a love story this time, but a thriller where the characters, Blake and Rik - or Kaleb and

Kir as he would name them - come to a very unfortunate end.

Stella

Footprint

Stella closed down her computer, pulled her workbag out from under her desk and took out her phone. *Popping 2 shop on way home. Do u want anything?*

Dave never answered his texts straight away. She'd check her messages once she was on the bus. As she put her phone back into her bag, something seemed not quite right. Her keys weren't there. It was the second time this week they'd gone missing. Admittedly, the first time she obviously hadn't looked properly because when she checked her bag later, they were in the front pocket. Stella never put her keys in the front pocket, but with everything else that had been happening lately, she must have done so absent mindedly. Shaking the contents of her bag out onto her desk, she rifled through the pile in front of her, picking out some old shopping lists and supermarket receipts before putting them in the wastepaper basket. She couldn't find anything with all those bits of paper cluttering things. After checking her bag, including the front pocket, was completely empty, she put back her purse and phone, as well as a packet of mints, lipstick, and two photographs: one of herself with her baby daughter, and another of Rosie on her first day at school. But there were no keys.

'Is there a problem? You look a bit flustered,' Justin, her colleague said.

'No. Everything's fine, thanks.'

The last thing Stella wanted was for Justin to think she was careless. He'd been earmarked for the account manager's role she'd been appointed to as an outside candidate and was quick to point out, at every opportunity, that he had far more experience with the company than she did. He'd been even more unbearable today after being passed over for promotion a second time yesterday. He was certain the assistant manager's post was in the bag, and his interview was just a formality. When the position was offered to Abby, who also worked in the office, the colour of his face was such that Stella was on the verge of phoning for one of the office first-aiders.

Pushing in her chair, Stella picked her bag up off her desk and slung it over her shoulder. Her keys were bound to turn up, eventually. Perhaps she'd left them at home? She retraced her steps in her mind. Dave worked from home on a Thursday. She'd kissed him and Rosie goodbye. They'd waved her off on the doorstep. She was running late and only had five minutes to get to the bus stop. Yes, that's what must have happened. She was sure they'd be there on the key hook in the hall when she got home.

'Off already?' Justin looked away from his screen and pushed his glasses up onto his head.

'Yes.' Stella lifted her jacket from the coat-stand and placed it over the crook of her arm. Searching for her keys had made her late, but she wouldn't give him the satisfaction by pointing that out. 'See you tomorrow.' *Worse luck.*

Out in the corridor, she pressed the button for the lift; with the office being on one of the middle floors of the high-rise office block, it was already full when it stopped on her floor. As the doors opened, Emily from HR stepped out.

'Oh, hi Stella. You're late tonight,' she said, looking at her wristwatch.

What a difference to Justin, Stella thought. Emily must have been almost twenty years younger than herself, yet she'd been the one conducting the interview when Stella had been appointed. In fact, Emily had been the one who'd told her she should apply for the post. Stella was working as manager of a coffee shop, *The Story Collector,* at the time. Emily had been a regular customer, often making time to talk to Stella and ask how she was. She had such a vibrancy about her and Stella couldn't help but feel a connection to her, admiring the way she made her own decisions and took charge of her own life; something Stella wished she'd had the chance to do when she was younger.

Everybody in the lift squeezed up to let Stella in, but as she was about to step inside an overwhelming sense of claustrophobia hit her; the heat of the office faded into insignificance compared to the mixed body odour radiating from the lift. A burning heat spun through her. Wet patches were breaking through her blouse, under her arms and across her back. She caught a glimpse of herself in the lift's mirror and barely recognised the red shiny face staring back at her.

'Sorry. Wrong button.' Walking down several flights of stairs was preferable to the hemmed-in walls of the lift.

A knot of anxiety swirled around in her stomach

as she thought about how she'd misplaced her keys. Again. She'd heard stories of women becoming forgetful during the menopause and hoped this wasn't the first in a line of forgetful episodes ahead of her. At least it would be Friday tomorrow, and then the weekend. Her mind wandered to the tea-party she'd planned for Rosie's sixth birthday on Sunday. A lot of the parents of the children in Rosie's class hired ball-pits or the local sports hall, complete with bouncy castles and magicians, or took the entire class bowling. But Rosie just wanted eight of her friends from school to come for tea where they'd make their own pizza, cookies, and cupcakes. Stella would also invite a handful of close friends and family, to give her a helping hand at the birthday party and to relax with a family barbecue and a couple of bottles of fizz, once Rosie's classmates had gone home.

Rosie was six months old when she came to live with Stella and Dave. Her mother just sixteen years old, thrown onto the streets by her step-mother and barely able to take care of herself let alone a baby. They'd fostered Rosie at first, but as time went on it was clear Rosie's birth mother wanted nothing to do with her. When people found out that Stella and Dave had adopted Rosie, they often told her how admirable they were, and how terrible it was that Rosie's birth mother had abandoned her. But Stella didn't see it that way; she knew just how vulnerable Rosie's poor mother must have been to be in that situation at such a young age and how brave she'd been to keep her daughter for six months before handing her over to social services.

Stella's bus stopped right outside the supermarket. Dave had texted back, saying to pick up a couple of steaks to throw on the barbecue later. Stella also needed to pick up a photo frame. She'd arrived home earlier in the week to find the cat had knocked the photograph of Dave, Rosie, and herself off the mantlepiece, and the glass had shattered into tiny shards. After making her way towards the check-out, Stella saw an offer she couldn't refuse. Prosecco only six pounds. What a bargain and just what she needed after a stressful couple of days.

Arriving home, Stella could hear Rosie playing in the garden. Unlatching the side gate, she walked around to the back garden. Dave was sitting outside at the patio table reading a book, whilst Rosie bounced away on the trampoline, and the cat lay sunning itself on the grass. The south-facing garden meant the heat was intense, but with the sun starting to dip, the early evening was one of the best parts of the day.

'Mummy.' Rosie waved from the trampoline. 'Look what I can do.' Rosie somersaulted into the air, filling Stella with pride at what a happy and confident little girl she was becoming.

'Hey, babes.' Dave stood up and gave Stella a kiss.

'Hi, darling. I'll just pop this in the fridge, then I'll be out to join you.'

Stella walked into the kitchen, put the shopping away, then made her way to the hall. She hung up her jacket, dropped her work bag on the floor, and kicked off her shoes. Her keys weren't on the hook. She'd have a proper look for them later. What she needed right now was a glass of fizz to quench her thirst. Returning to the kitchen, she poured a beaker of orange for Rosie, and filled two champagne flutes with Prosecco; one for her and one for Dave.

'Another bottle of wine? Stressful week?' Dave asked as she joined him in the garden.

'I'll have you know this is the first I've had this week, cheeky.' She mockingly slapped his thigh.

'Um, have you forgotten about the one we were saving for our meal on Saturday?'

'What do you mean "were"?'

'Well, it's not in the fridge, so unless our

daughter has drunk it, which is extremely unlikely seeing as she doesn't know how to pop a cork, then that means you must have.'

'I don't know what you're talking about,' Stella said.

'Hey, it's okay. Two bottles in a week is no big deal, you work hard babes.'

Stella considered whether the menopause was making her forgetful. It wasn't like Dave to make things up, and it must be one of the two.

The next morning, Rosie came downstairs, already dressed in her school uniform. *I'm so lucky to have such a good little girl,* Stella thought. Things were much different these days, of course, but she hoped that Rosie would grow up to make good life choices for herself. Above all, she knew that whatever curveballs life threw at her daughter, then she'd be there to support her no matter what.

After breakfast, and making sure Rosie had everything she needed for her school day, Stella brushed Rosie's hair into a ponytail with her Peppa Pig hairbrush, then looked around for her own brush. She always kept it next to Rosie's hairbrush, but it had been missing for a couple of days now. She moved the magazine, but it wasn't under there. She looked on the floor and down the back of the unit. But she couldn't find it anywhere. Time was getting on; she would just have to use Rosie's Peppa Pig brush again until she was able to buy herself a new one.

Stella arrived at the office, going straight to the kitchen area to make herself a cup of coffee. Emily was there.

'Got to get my priorities right,' she said, holding up a mugful of coffee. 'Can't start my day without a brew.'

'Definitely,' Stella agreed. There was something familiar about Emily; the way her cheeks dimpled when she smiled, and the way she shook her hair out of her eyes as if it annoyed her. *Who does she remind me of?* Stella thought.

Stella made her way to her desk, disappointed to see Justin had already arrived. With the company offering flexible working times, he usually started work a bit later, and Stella's early morning cup of coffee without Justin's annoying disapproval was the best part of the day. Now he'd spoiled it by arriving first. It wasn't that Justin objected to caffeine, he just insisted on taking his on structured breaks away from his desk, and expected Stella to follow the same office routine that he'd done over the years. Stella being his line manager was a concept that seemed to have escaped Justin. Switching on her computer with one hand, Stella opened her desk drawer with the other and reached for her notepad and pen. She didn't want that going missing by leaving it out on her desk overnight; Justin had a habit of borrowing her stationery and not returning it. She was just about to close the drawer when something caught her eye. It was her special keyring of her baby daughter's footprint, and attached to that were her keys. *What the hell were they doing in there?* Rage burst through her. She'd had her suspicions that Justin had been trying to undermine her position by making her appear forgetful, and now this confirmed things. There was no way she'd put them in her drawer, and nobody except Justin had the motive or opportunity. He must have taken them from her bag whilst she was away from her desk yesterday.

'Is there something you need to tell me?' She tried her utmost to keep calm.

'Oh yes,' Justin replied. 'Emily from HR was sitting at your desk when I came in. She said she found your keys in the lift last night. She wants you to go and see her. I asked her what it was about but she wouldn't say.'

Stella thought about how she could have lost her keys in the lift. She'd carried her jacket over her arm. Had she put them in her pocket earlier that day, and they'd fallen out when she left the office that evening? *Yes, that must be what happened.* Although she couldn't remember putting her keys in her pocket. She always put her keys in her bag. Why would she have put them in her jacket pocket? But that couldn't be right - she couldn't have dropped them in the lift because she didn't get in.

Stella decided to ask Emily about it later. She didn't trust Justin, but now there was an element of doubt and she didn't want to make herself look stupid if he turned out to be innocent. She put her hand in the drawer to lift out the keys, but as she did so, her hand caught on something else. Her hairbrush; the one she only ever kept at home on the hall table. But there were fewer hairs; she'd been meaning to clean it but hadn't got around to it.

'Actually,' Justin carried on. 'You and that Emily don't half look alike. You have the mannerisms too; the way you both shake your hair out of your eyes. What with her giving you the job and everything, a more suspicious person might think you're related or something.'

Stella looked at her keyring of the baby's

footprint. But it didn't belong to Rosie. It belonged to the baby she was cuddling in the photograph; the one she kept with her always - in her bag alongside the photograph of Rosie on her first day at school. Sweat trickled down her back as she felt the heat rise from her chest and up her neck until it burned into her cheeks. Justin's face swam out of focus as the floor came up towards her, before spiralling back to where it belonged. A feeling she had become all too familiar with over the last few months, but this time it wasn't middle age that was to blame. It was her teenage years that had finally caught up with her.

Emily

The Boyfriend

Emily scrolled through the photos on her phone. *Everything had been so perfect back then,* she thought as she looked at the photo of Stacey and herself laid out on sun-loungers, sipping cocktails at the side of the pool in Turkey. Being born only one week apart, the flatmates had gone away to celebrate their twenty-fifth birthdays; and with both women having recently split from their respective boyfriends, romance was the last thing on their minds.

It was the second day of the holiday and Emily and Stacey were out on the hotel's balcony nursing their hangovers with extra-strong black coffees, when in a half-asleep and still slightly nauseous state, they heard a male voice in their own familiar West Country accent.

'Alright, ladies. Looks like it's gonna be a hot one today.' It was one of the men staying in the room next door, standing there in his shorts, flaunting his tanned six-pack.

'Sure is.' Stacey eyed him up and down. 'And the temperature's just gone up a few degrees.'

It wasn't long before the women were spending their days (and nights) with the two men, who they'd discovered were called Ed and Rik. And their plan to keep men off their holiday agenda soon became a distant memory as they embraced their holiday flings. But on the last night of the holiday, whilst Stacey and Ed spent the night saying their goodbyes in Ed's hotel room, Emily and Rik were left alone to stroll along the cool, sandy beach. Buzz of the busy daytime replaced with a sense of tranquillity. As the Aegean Sea ebbed and flowed at their feet, Rik stopped in his tracks and turned to face Emily.

'This has been the best holiday, I've ever had,' he said, pulling her in closer.

'Me too.' Emily placed her head on his shoulder before looking up at him as their lips met.

'I don't want this to end,' Rik said, as their lips parted.

'Nor me.' Emily's heart was racing. Finding Mr Right was the last thing on her mind a week ago, but now it seemed he was right here in front of her.

'Then we shouldn't let the end of our holiday be the end of us. It's not like we live at opposite ends of the country. Even if we did, that shouldn't stop us. I like you, Emily. I mean, I really like you.'

Back in England, the more time Emily spent with Rik, the more she found herself falling for him. It wasn't long before it wasn't just weekends that he didn't bother going back to his own home overnight. Although the flat belonged to Emily, Stacey had been her flatmate for as long as Emily could remember. But if two was company, then three was becoming a crowd. After Stacey used Rik's razor to shave her legs and arm-pits, as well as God knows what other body parts, Emily had no choice but to tell Stacey it was time she found a place of her own.

Five months later, Stacey still wasn't speaking to Emily. To top it all, Rik had stormed out earlier, following a row she'd had with him about his dodgy whereabouts over the last few weeks. She knew Rik had been a bit of a lad before they'd met. Hanging around with his mate, Blake; but since he'd become friends with Ed, he'd grown away from Blake and his immature pranks on women. But now she was worried whether she was too boring for him.

Emily closed the photo app and put her phone down on the coffee table. The last she'd heard was that Stacey was staying in Carla's spare room. Carla was Stacey's super-tidy OCD sister who went ballistic if you so much as ruffled the cushions on her sofa or left a used coffee cup in the kitchen sink – and that was just for guests.

'At least I have you,' Emily said to Suky, as her tabby cat jumped onto her lap. 'But, unless I want to turn into a lonely old cat lady, then it's about time I took matters into my own hands and sorted things out with Stacey.'

A stab of guilt hit Emily. Would Stacey think she was only getting back in touch because she'd fallen out with Rik? If she was honest, she couldn't be sure of it herself. But one thing she knew was that Rik storming off was the catalyst for accepting that the rift between her and Stacey was all her fault. She wouldn't blame Stacey if she told her to get lost, but a reconciliation would never happen unless one of them made the first move.

Lifting Suky off her lap, Emily took her jacket from the hook in the hall and made her way to Carla's house. It was a cool, dry day and the twenty-minute walk would give her time to plan what she was going to say when she got there.

Approaching the house, Emily could see Stacey's bright blue Toyota parked outside. *Good, at least she's in.* But as Emily opened the garden gate, she couldn't help but notice the Red BMW parked in front of Stacey's car. Rik's car. *What was he doing here?* Emily slammed the gate and marched down the path. She banged hard on the door before ringing the bell. There was no answer. She tried again. Knocking so hard her knuckles hurt. Still no answer. Emily was about to walk away when she noticed the curtain in the living room twitch.

'I know you're in there,' she called through the letterbox before slamming it down as hard as she could.

The curtains twitched again before a tabby cat appeared in the windowsill. It was Jess, Suky's mother. Knowing how much Emily loved cats but had never had one of her own, Stacey had surprised Emily with Suky when she was feeling particularly fed up after another failed attempt at searching for her birthmother. And Emily wouldn't have traced her birthmother, Stella, at all, had it not been for Stacey's detective skills, where she found Stella working in a coffee shop. *How did things get this bad?* Emily thought. They'd been such good friends, always looking out for each other and cheering each other up when one of them came to the end of a relationship. They never used to let men come between them, but now Stacey was virtually homeless because Emily had put Rik first. Now it looked like Emily was destined to be single, with just her cat for company, because Stacey had committed the ultimate sin and stolen Rik away from her.

Emily had come here to apologise, prepared to accept everything was her fault, but what Stacey had done was far worse. And Stacey didn't even have the courage to face her. Emily thought about all the times she'd been piggy in the middle when Stacey and Rik had fallen out over petty arguments. Was it all just a ruse to put her off the scent? Were they both inside the house laughing at her?

'She's not in, my love.' The woman next door had come out to sort her recycling. 'I saw her leave earlier with that man who's been here quite a bit lately. Shall I tell her who called?'

'No, it's okay. I was just calling about... about um... some new windows. Those new triple glazed ones.'

'Oh, that's nice. Actually, I was thinking of having a new window installed in my kitchen. Do you think you could help me with that?'

'Um. Sorry, we don't do kitchen windows.'

'Really? Why not?'

'Kitchen windows have special… um, special seals. Sorry.'

A lump formed in Emily's throat. Although she'd been angry with Rik, she still thought they'd sort things out; eventually. She never guessed in a million years that his mysterious disappearances over the last few weeks were because he'd been seeing Stacey behind her back. *Well, good riddance to both of them,* she thought, annoyed with herself for being prepared to apologise to Stacey and take the blame for everything.

Emily walked out of the gate and saw Stacey and Rik's cars parked nose to nose as if they were kissing. Rik's BMW was his pride and joy, the tiniest smudge of dirt and he was out there polishing it. *Well, polish this out, Rik.* She scraped her key down the side of both doors. *And you too, whilst I'm at it.* Emily did the same to Stacey's beloved Toyota.

Emily had just sat down in front of the TV when Rik arrived home.

'Sorry I went off in a huff earlier babe,' he said, as he kissed her on the cheek. 'I've just been a bit stressed that's all. And now some loser has gone and scratched my car.'

'That's terrible.' Emily twirled her hair around her fingers before chewing the ends. 'Where did that happen?'

'When I was out with Ed.' Emily watched Rik carefully; waiting for him to twist the small silver earring he wore in his ear. A habit he had when he was nervous. Instead, he came over and sat next to her. 'So, what have you been up to?'

'Oh, nothing much. Just had a lazy Sunday and stayed in with Suky. Didn't I Sukes?'

Suky jumped up onto Rik's lap and meowed.

'I think she's telling tales on you.' Rik laughed as he gently nudged Emily with his elbow. 'Look, I'm sorry I've been neglecting you lately. I thought that tomorrow night we could go out to Chiovani's, that Italian place you love. A special treat on me.'

Emily remembered how her ex-boyfriend used to give her flowers; and how naïve she was, believing he wanted to spoil her because he loved her so much. Then she found out the flowers coincided with the times he'd cheated on her. She'd thought Rik was different, but it looked like Emily had got things wrong yet again. Well, she wasn't going to put up with it any longer. Chiovani's was her absolute favourite restaurant, but it wasn't cheap. And they did Bollinger. She'd make sure she'd have the most expensive thing on the menu - and wash it down with Champagne. Then she'd tell him she knew what a cheat he was.

The next day was Monday and Emily's boss, Linda, was away at a conference all week. Emily usually looked forward to her being away from the office, but this time Linda had delegated all her meetings to Emily. And that meant visiting the company's other branch on the other side of town. The morning went well; getting away from her place of work and meeting people that she usually only spoke to on the telephone made the morning go by much quicker than Emily expected, and by lunchtime she was starving.

'There's a great sandwich bar just around the corner,' one of her colleagues told her. 'The one near the park.'

'Perfect,' Emily said. It would be a change to have lunch in the park instead of a stuffy office.

The baguettes looked delicious. She was tempted but didn't want to spoil her appetite for later. She had every intention of having a starter and a pudding at Chiovani's. After selecting a chicken and avocado wrap, and an Americano coffee, Emily made her way to the park. There was also a children's play area, some swings, a climbing frame, and a helter-skelter type slide. Two young children were kicking a ball about with their mother. Emily placed her coffee on the floor just under the bench and took out her chicken wrap. As she did so, one of the children kicked the ball, sending it in Emily's direction and knocking over the coffee.

'I'm so sorry.' It was the woman that Emily had assumed was the children's mother. 'Emily!'

'Stacey. I didn't recognise you. Your hair really suits you that colour. And the cut.'

'Thanks.' Stacey pulled her fingers through her bright blonde pixie cut, so it spiked up. 'It's more practical like this, chasing around after the children. But what are you doing here?'

'I'm working at the other branch today, just around the corner.' Emily pointed towards the office. 'What about you? These aren't the usual children you look after.'

'No. I don't work for the doctor and his wife now; they moved back to London. I'm nannying for a new family, which has worked out really well because I get to live in.'

'You don't live with Carla anymore, then?'

'No. She was too much of a pain in the arse with all her cushions and stuff. And it would have been totally weird living there under the circumstances.'

'You must still see her, though. I thought I saw your car there the other day?'

'Well, I do, but it's not my car anymore. I get to use the Land Rover that belongs to the family I work for, so I let Carla have my old car. Bit of a thank you for letting me stay there when I had nowhere else to go.'

It all made sense now. Rik was much more suited to Carla with their obsessively tidy habits. The thought of Rik cheating on her still made her want to never trust another man ever again, but it was a relief to know he hadn't cheated with her best friend. Or ex-best friend as she was now, thanks to Emily's stupidity.

'About what happened. I'm really sorry, Stace. I shouldn't have made you move out.'

'Look, I'm not pretending that it didn't upset me, you putting Rik before me and all that. But it was the kick up the bum I needed. Moving in with Carla made me realise what a slob I was. And if I hadn't been living with Carla then I might not have applied for the job I have now.' Stacey sat down on the bench next to Emily. 'I'd love it if we could put everything behind us.'

Emily looked at her friend. Did Stacey know

about Rik and Carla? It seemed that way. What else could she have meant by it being weird living there under the circumstances? Was Stacey just trying to prove a point that Rik was a loser? But what if Stacey was genuine and Emily pushed her away? Then there would be no way back for their friendship. She had to take the chance.

'I'd like that,' Emily said.

That evening, Emily spent twice as long as normal preening herself to perfection. It was about time Rik realised what a mistake he'd made. At least now she knew it was Carla he was seeing rather than Stacey like she first thought, and she wouldn't be making a fool of herself with false accusations.

'Wow. You look absolutely gorgeous,' he told her as they made their way out to the car.

'Thanks. You don't look so bad yourself.' Emily's tummy flipped over at the sight of Rik in the jeans she'd bought him for his birthday a couple of weeks ago, which he was wearing with his favourite black shirt. And he was wearing Boss. He knew she couldn't resist him when he wore it. *Bastard!*

As they arrived at Chiovani's, Emily was reminded of all the good times they'd had there. Her eyes watered as she realised this would be the last time they'd come here together. She wiped the stray tear away. There was no way she was going to allow her makeup to run. She needed to look her absolute best tonight.

'Hello. I have a table booked in the name of Rik Green.' Rik told the maître d'.

'Of course, sir; madam.' The maître d' led Emily and Rik to one of the large circular tables in the centre of the room. He pulled out a chair and gestured for Emily to sit down before pouring them both a glass of water from the bottle in the centre of the table. 'Is there anything I can get you while you wait, sir?'

'No. Thank you. If we could just have five minutes alone. Please.'

'What's going on, Rik? Wait for what? Why are we sat at this big table when there are smaller ones over there?'

'Em, there's something I need to tell you before...' Rik looked around the room before playing with his earring. 'Promise you won't be mad at me.'

This wasn't what Emily was expecting at all. She was planning on doing the dumping not being dumped, but she wasn't about to make things easy for him by telling him she already knew what he was going to say.

'Go on,' she said.

'I haven't been going to the gym these last few weeks.'

'Really? You don't say.'

'Look, you'll find out what I've been up to soon enough, but I just want you to know that I love you. And even if you get mad at me, you should know that I've had your best interests at heart.'

'How could you cheating on me possibly be in my best interest?'

'Cheating on you? What on earth are you talking about? You know I'm crazy about you.'

Emily was about to tell Rik that she knew all about his secret liaisons with Carla when she saw Ed walk into the restaurant and over to their table.

'Alright mate,' he said, slapping Rik on the back. 'Alright Em.' He pulled out the chair next to Rik before sitting down. 'So, how are things?'

But before Rik or Emily could answer him, Emily was stunned to see Stacey and Carla walk into the restaurant. Not only that, they were walking over to their table.

'Hello, darling.' Carla walked up to Ed and kissed him on the lips before sitting next to him. 'Hi, Rik. Hi Emily. It's good to see you both.'

'Hi, hun.' Stacey said as she sat in the empty seat

next to Emily. 'We don't see each other for like ages, then it's twice in one day. Sorry I didn't say anything about this earlier, but I was sworn to secrecy.'

Rik reached over and touched Emily's hand. 'I'm sorry babe, tricking you like this, but it was the only way I knew I could be sure you'd agree to come.'

'What's going on?' Emily asked. 'Is this some kind of musical boyfriends' game?' She looked at Carla and Ed, then to Stacey, then finally back to Rik.

'What, Carla and Ed?' Stacey said. 'I know. I couldn't believe it when I found out. Ed had no idea that Carla was my sister when they met. As you know, it was never anything other than a holiday fling between us, but it was still weird seeing the two of them together. It was one of the reasons I took my new job as a live-in nanny.'

'Carla was the one who said just how unhappy Stacey had been since you two fell out,' Rik told Emily. 'We've been putting our heads together to come up with a way to get you two back together again. That's where I've been these last few weeks, over at Carla and Ed's place. Except for yesterday afternoon when we went over to Stacey's new place to explain what we'd been up to. I needed to make sure Stacey was on board before letting you in on my plan. I didn't want to get your hopes up if Stacey wasn't interested in making things up with you.'

'So, you really were with Ed yesterday?'

'Yes. Of course, I was. I know I didn't tell you exactly where I'd been, but I'd never tell you an outright lie, babes.' Rik reached into the pocket of his suit jacket. 'It's been almost a year since we met in Turkey. As you know, for me it was the most magical holiday I could have wished for. But as amazing as it was, I know you and Stacey went away to spend time together before Ed and I came along. I feel terrible about coming between the pair of you, so I want you to have this.' Rik handed Emily an email confirming a holiday for two at the same resort in Turkey. 'It's for you and Stacey.'

'I don't know what to say. I was convinced that... Well, it doesn't matter now.'

'Oh, before I forget,' Ed said, as he turned to Carla. 'I saw Paula, next door, earlier. I asked her about the car.'

'About the car?' Stacey said.

'Yes. Sorry, Stacey,' Carla said. 'As you know we drove over to your place in Ed's car, and whilst we were gone Rik's Beamer and the Toyota were targeted by some moron who left big scratches down the side of both of them.'

'No. Not my old Toyota. I loved that little car.'

'Well, hopefully, we'll find the culprit.' Ed poured himself some water from the bottle that the waiter had placed in the centre of the table earlier. 'Paula said there was this dodgy woman selling double glazing, so she's invited us to go round and look at her CCTV later.'

~~~

Paula

Friend or Foe?

Paula placed a mug of tea on the kitchen table in front of her younger sister, Jodi, before sitting down. 'I'm so worried about her Jode. I know teenagers like to spend time in their rooms, but it's getting beyond a joke now. It was so much easier when Zoe was little. Teenagers are such hard work.'

'I wouldn't worry too much, sis. Mum used to say the same about me. Some people just prefer their own company. I still do. If it wasn't for taking Patsy to nursery, and our writing group, I don't think I'd get out at all.'

'I know what you mean. I don't know what I'd do without our writing friends. You're reading your poem out tonight, aren't you ?'

'Yes. I still need to tweak it a bit, though. It's

been tough writing about something so personal. I want to make sure every word is the right choice.'

'I'm sure it will be wonderful. You're a brilliant writer. Not every mother has an immediate bond with their baby. It will resonate with a lot of mothers.'

'Do you think so? '

'I know so. Look I'm just gonna go and check on Zoe. It's not like her to shut herself away like this. That will give you some quiet space to finish it.'

Paula knocked on her daughter's bedroom door. 'Is it okay to come in Zo?'

'No.'

'Zo, don't be like that. Come on, let me in.'

'Seriously, just get off my back.' Zoe opened the door before stomping across her bedroom and laying back down on her bed. 'I told you, I'm not going to school ever again.'

'A lot of people are really worried about you, you know.' Paula walked across the room and sat on the edge of her teenage daughter's bed.

'Like who? You and Dad, you mean.' Zoe rolled over onto her side, facing away from Paula. She scrunched up her pillow before tucking it under her neck.

'Yes, me and Dad. Your friends, too. Maddy has

been ringing the house phone, says you're ignoring her calls and texts.'

'Like I care what she thinks.'

'Come on Zo. You've been friends since reception class. What's going on?'

'I hate her. I don't want to talk about it.'

'I'm always here to listen, sweetheart, you know that.' Paula reached over and ran her fingers through her daughter's long dark hair, brushing it back off her face.

'You'll just take her side. Like everyone does. Miss goody-two-shoes. She makes me sick.'

'She is a bit, isn't she? I've always thought that. The way her mother panders to her is so irritating. It's no wonder she's turned out to be so spoiled.'

Zoe turned over and sat up, bending her knees and hugging them like a comfort blanket. 'But I thought you and Auntie Sally were like total besties.'

'Even best friends fall out sometimes.'

'She copied my essay, Mum. And I got the blame. All the teachers think she's so perfect, that she'd never do anything wrong. Nobody believes me, but she did and it's so unfair. And now she's best friends with Lucy, who like just lets her copy her work so she'll be her friend.'

'Well, I'm sure Lucy's parents won't be too

pleased to hear that.'

'No, you can't say anything, Mum. Everybody will think I'm a snitch and hate me even more than they do already.'

'I won't say anything if you don't want me to, darling. And don't worry, this will all be forgotten in a few days, believe me.'

'I know.' Zoe moved closer to her mother and gave her a hug. 'Thanks, Mum. But what I don't get is that Lucy is really popular. She has loads of other friends. And I thought she liked me.'

'Well, it's not worth worrying about. Are you coming down?' Paula held out her hands to give her daughter a helping hand off the bed. 'Auntie Jodi is here.'

'How was your day, Auntie Jodie?' Zoe asked as they were sitting at the kitchen table.

'It was my turn to help out at Patsy's nursery this morning.'

'I bet Patsy liked that, having you there.'

'Yes, she did. But she loves nursery anyway. Her play leader is lovely. You might know her daughter actually; she's the same age as you and goes to your school. Lisa Davidson. She's won loads of medals for ice skating.' Jodie added the final word to her poem and put her pen down to give her niece her full attention.

'I know a Lucy Davidson.' Zoe said.

'Yes, that's it. Lucy. Are you friends? From what her mum says about her, I can imagine you two getting on.'

'We're kind of friends. She's got a great sense of humour. I think that's why she's so popular.'

'Haha, yes, she sounds a bit like her mum. In fact it was her mum's idea to trick this girl who tried to copy Lucy's history homework.'

Zoe and her mother looked at each other.

'Sounds like she deserved it,' said Paula.

'Too right. Lucy's a clever little thing, by all accounts. Not just with those ice skates, but academically too. A bit like you, Zo.' Jodi picked up a biscuit from the plate in the centre of the table and took a small bite. 'This other girl had a right cheek. Mandy I think her name is.'

'It's Maddy.'

'Really, that's a coincidence. Your mate's called Maddy as well, isn't she?'

'Yes.'

Paula looked at Zoe as they gave each other a knowing smile.

'Anyway, Lucy isn't just clever, she's pretty

cunning too.' Jodi picked up her pen and pressed the top of her ballpoint pen on and off a couple of times. 'She wrote her own essay as normal. And then wrote another one, which was total nonsense, for this Maddy girl. They get the results back tomorrow. I'd just love to see the look on the girl's face when she finds out she's been had.'

'No,' Zoe said. 'Neither can I. Actually, I'm quite looking forward to going to school tomorrow.'

~~~

Kirsty

Her Blood Sister

The herby aroma wafting from the kitchen welcomes me the moment I walk through the door, reminding me of our family holiday in Rome. Mum has cooked some sort of Bolognese combination once a week ever since. Spag bol one Wednesday, lasagne the next. Our mid-week comfort food to see us through to the weekend. But today is Monday; we usually have lamb chops on a Monday. I don't like lamb chops.

'Hello, Kirsty, love. How's your day been?' Mum says as she places slices of garlic bread onto a baking sheet.

'Parts of it were good,' I say. 'We found a home for that cute Staffy that was abandoned a couple of weeks ago. But we had a gorgeous litter of six puppies brought in whose mother died giving birth.'

71

Unfortunately, it's not unusual to have abandoned litters brought into the animal rescue centre where I've worked since leaving sixth form college last year, but there's something about these puppies that have got to me. Especially the smallest one, a little girl that I got to name. I've decided to call her Lottie, after Charlotte Bronte, my absolute all-time favourite author.

'Oh darling, that is sad. Never mind, I'm sure you'll find suitable homes for them all.'

My boss, Tina, said I could have Lottie when she's ready to leave the animal rescue centre, as long as Mum and Dad agree. I'm pretty sure Mum will agree, but Dad will only agree if Mum does. I need to get her on my side first, and then she can talk Dad around. I try to find the right moment, but my sister, Maddy, is hogging Mum's attention, whispering to her about something.

'Shoot!' Mum cries, as a slice of bread slips from her hand and onto the floor.

'It's okay Mum, let me do it,' Maddy offers.

'Have I entered some kind of parallel world or something?' I say, taking the cutlery out of the kitchen drawer and walking over to the dining table. Maddy, who has just turned sixteen and is three years younger than me, never helps. It's always Kirsty do this, Kirsty do that, never Maddy. She just sits there slumped in front of the TV, looking smug. When I ask 'why me?' Mum says it's because I'm the eldest; like that's a valid reason.

'I'm not totally useless, you know.' Maddy places the tray of bread into the oven and walks over to help me set the table, which is possibly the first time ever.

Mum brings over a big bowl of salad and places it on the table and we hear Dad's key in the door as he arrives home. I see Maddy look over at Mum, and she gives her that *don't worry, everything will be alright* look, that she does when one of us is in trouble. Something is going on; I just know it is.

'So, what has she done this time?' I ask.

'It's nothing,' Mum says. 'Zoe accused Maddy of copying her homework and they've had a falling out, that's all. You know what teenage girls are like. You were the same at that age.'

'Um, I don't think I was that bad,' I say.

But Mum stops what she is doing and gives me another of her special looks that says *oh yes, you were.* 'It will all blow over, but me and Paula have had a few words about it. She seems to think Zoe is innocent in all of this. I'm not having her blaming Maddy for everything, not after what she's been through.'

I'm just about to ask what she means when Dad enters the kitchen.

'How are my girls? Everything all okay?' Dad gives Mum a peck on the cheek like he always does, but I sense a nervous edge. He's still wearing his shoes, which he usually leaves in the hall, and Mum hasn't even told him to take them off, let alone shout at him for making a mess of her clean floor. There's more to things than Maddy falling out with Zoe, and Mum falling out with Paula, I just know there is.

'We're all good,' Maddy says.

I can't stop thinking about the orphaned puppies and feel far from good, but I'm saving my energy for what I have to ask my parents later.

Dad walks over and kisses me on top of the head, then Maddy. Maddy might get away with things with Mum, but there's no question that I'm Dad's favourite. I think of asking him about the puppy but decide to wait until he's eaten his dinner and had his daily tipple of whiskey. If I ask now, he would no doubt only say 'ask your mother'.

'This is nice. Bolognese on a Monday,' Dad says as we all sit down at the dining table for dinner.

Mum doesn't have to say anything. The way she narrows her eyes and pinches her lips at him is enough.

'Right, what's going on?' I ask. I bet it's got something to do with Maddy. That would be typical of her to get herself pregnant or something, so we won't be allowed to have a puppy.

'You know Dad and I love you and Maddy both the same.' Mum sets her fork and spoon back down onto the table.

I know this isn't strictly true. Mum loves Maddy a bit more than she loves me, and Dad loves me a bit more than he loves Maddy. But I give her the benefit of the doubt and let her continue.

'You and Maddy both love each other too. You'd do anything for each other, wouldn't you?' It wasn't a question; she really thinks we would. Parents are strange like that.

'She's not having my room; she will have to squeeze a cot in her room.' I'm putting my foot down on this one.

'What has your room and a cot got to do with anything?' Mum asks. She stands up and walks over to the dresser, picking something up before returning to the table. She sits back in her seat before pushing a photo of Auntie Barbara, her dead sister, in front of me.

Oh my God, it's not my room she wants, she's

dying and wants one of my kidneys or something. I look over at Maddy, who is loading her plate with garlic bread; she's quieter than usual, but it doesn't look like there's anything wrong with her.

'I loved my sister very much,' Mum continues. 'There wasn't anything that I wouldn't do for her.'

'I know,' I say.

'What you don't know is that Auntie Barbara was twenty-one weeks pregnant when she found out she had cancer and had two choices: abort her child and have chemotherapy or risk it and put treatment off until after the birth.'

'Oh my God, Mum, that's terrible. Poor Auntie Barbara having to go through a termination when she was already so ill.' I wonder if that's it? Has my sister had a termination? A stab of guilt hits me for being so selfish. A smaller room would have been no price to pay.

'No, Auntie Barbara went ahead with the pregnancy. Her baby daughter was just eight weeks old when she died.'

Maddy's eyes water and she scrubs away an escaped tear. Dad reaches over and places his hand over Maddy's. She looks even more like Mum when she cries. I look a bit like my mum, but mostly like my dad.

'That must have been hard for the baby being torn away from her mother just as she was getting to know her. But then I guess at least she would have been too young to remember after a while. Like puppies, they're taken from their mothers at eight weeks.'

Maddy shoots a hard look at me. 'It's not quite the same thing, stupid.'

'So, we have a cousin then,' I say. 'What happened to her, was she adopted or something?'

'Yes. You'd only just had your third birthday when she was adopted.'

'So, she must be about Maddy's age then.'

'Yes, she's exactly the same age as Maddy.'

'I bet she's not half as annoying though.'

Used to our sibling rivalry bickering, Mum carries on. 'As you know, Auntie Barbara never married. Social services were ready to take her daughter into care.'

'That's horrible. Wasn't there anybody who could look after her?'

'Yes.' Mum hands me another photograph. This time it's one of me holding Maddy when she was little. The proud big sister, planting a kiss on her baby sister's forehead.

'There was no way I was going to let that

happen. All of us had already fallen in love with little Maddy, especially you.'

'So you mean…'

'We're not proper sisters,' Maddy finishes.

Relief pulses through me as I realise my pain in the arse sister isn't dying, but I'm too stunned to find anything intelligent to say. I pick up the photograph of Auntie Barbara. I've never noticed before how much Maddy looks like her.

'And that's why I'm the favourite.' Maddy gives me one of her sarcastic smiles. 'They chose me; you were just like conceived by Mum and Dad.'

I give my sister a kick under the table. She's such a pain in the arse, it's no wonder she fell out with Zoe. But although Maddy might well be joking, we both know there's an element of truth in what she says where our mother is concerned. Mum doesn't just see Maddy as her daughter, she also reminds her of the sister she's lost.

'We decided we'd put off telling you both until after Maddy's sixteenth birthday,' Mum says. 'We told, Maddy a few days ago but she wanted some time before we told you. She's worried you won't feel the same about her. But we need you both to know this changes nothing, you're still sisters.'

I look at my sister. For all her smart-arse

comments, I've never seen her looking so vulnerable. It's no wonder she tried to copy Zoe's homework. Her head must have been all over the place, she wouldn't have been able to concentrate. I feel an overwhelming sense of love for her. Mum was right, she's still my little sister.

'Is there anything you'd like to ask?' Dad says.

'Can we have a puppy?' I ask hopefully.

~~~

Colin

The Story Collector – Part 2

L iterature, Latte, and Love, was a huge success, reaching top spots in all the book charts. And Colin couldn't have been more proud when Lucas and Abby were married a few months after he'd sprinkled his literary magic over them.

There had been other developments in Colin's life, too. He'd known Stella for years, with her being the manager of his coffee shop before she worked at the office; but he'd no idea of the emotional pain she'd kept locked away. Like every year, Stella invited Colin and his wife to her daughter, Rosie's, birthday party. But this year, there was a special announcement, where Stella introduced Emily as the daughter she'd been forced to give up at birth. With Colin and his wife knowing Stella for many years, they'd already become surrogate grandparents to Rosie; and now Emily was also part of their extended family.

When Colin learned of Emily's relationship with Rik, he was torn in two. He knew what Rik had got up to in his past, but it appeared he'd moved on from his friendship with Blake. It was obvious how happy Emily had been since meeting him, and Colin's story where Blake and Rik (or Kaleb and Kir, as he'd planned on calling them) were killed in horrific circumstances, was scrapped. He'd have to go back to the drawing board – or his writing journal – to think of alternative fictional justice for Blake.

But just as Colin had accepted Rik as being a member of his unconventional family, Emily turned up on his doorstep in a distraught state, believing her relationship with Rik was about to come to an end. She'd made a huge mistake, and had vandalised Carla and Rik's cars, which was about to be revealed through Carla's neighbour's CCTV.

However, unbeknown to Emily, there was just one degree of separation in the chain of acquaintance between herself and Carla's neighbour. And Colin was that link. Colin knew how impulsive Emily could be, often finding herself in a tricky situation and then digging herself further into a hole. Like the time when she 'borrowed' Stella's keys to snoop around her house, then accidentally knocked over the photo frame. Then getting so stressed out at what she'd done, had helped herself to a glass of wine out of the fridge. Then another. But this time Colin could help.

Carla's neighbour, Paula, was a member of Colin's writing group, and she'd told Colin about how her daughter had fallen out with her best friend. In a heated moment, Paula had said some terrible things to Sally, the girl's mother; but when Paula discovered the reason behind the girl's behaviour, Paula had felt awful and wished she could retract what she'd said.

Colin knew it was a big favour asking Paula to delete the CCTV. But he also knew that if anybody was prepared to give somebody a second chance, then that person was Paula. After Colin explained Emily's situation, Paula agreed to delete the evidence on the condition that Emily promised not to take such drastic action in the future.

But in a similar way to Colin being the missing link between Emily and Paula, Paula was about to reconnect the link between Colin and somebody from his past.

At the writing group the following week, Colin asked Paula whether she'd patched things up with Sally. Paula told him that although things had been awkward between them for a while, they'd made amends when Sally's family adopted an orphaned puppy from the animal rescue centre where Sally's older daughter, Kirsty, worked. The puppy had far more energy than Sally had anticipated. When Sally arrived home from work each day, there was always something else that had been chewed up. And it wasn't fair keeping the puppy locked in a cage all day. Paula offered to pop in and check on the puppy when Sally was at work; letting her out into the garden and giving her some much-needed fuss.

Over the next few weeks, Paula shared pictures of Sally's new puppy on Facebook. When she posted a picture of when the puppy was first taken into the rescue centre compared to what it looked like now, Colin realised it was the same rescue centre where he'd adopted his own dog, Billie. Not only that, the woman at the centre who'd taken a shine to Billie after rescuing her from the stream when she was just six weeks old, still worked there. Her name was Tina, and if it hadn't been for her, Billie wouldn't have survived.

Commenting on Paula's picture, saying how lovely it was to see Tina after all this time. Colin subsequently received a friend request from her. But life hadn't been that great for Tina in recent months, and her posts centred around trying to find a suitable place to live. He remembered how difficult that had been for Abby and wondered whether if he wrote a story about Tina, then she too might find a happy ever after.

The following Sunday morning, Colin was sitting at one of the tables in *The Story Collector,* researching ideas for Tina's story over a cup of coffee.

'Is that another story you're writing, Colin?' It was Kate who worked as a part-time barista.

'Hopefully, it's the start of one,' Colin said. 'I'm just jotting down a few ideas.'

'Do you know what kind of stories, I like?' Kate said.

'Tell me,' Colin said as he pulled out a chair for her to sit down. 'I love to hear what other people think.'

'Stories where something in the past effects what happens in the future,' Kate said. 'Take me for example, if I hadn't missed the bus that morning then I wouldn't have walked to work. And if I hadn't walked to work then I wouldn't have bumped into the person who eventually became the surrogate to mine and Tom's baby.'

'Ah yes, cause and effect. It makes for a good story. In fact, I'm planning on an anachronic structure for this story.' Colin tapped his notebook with his pen.

'What's an anachronic structure?' Kate asked.

'It's where the storyline flits backwards and forwards between the past and the present. What happens in the past has a direct bearing on the present.'

'That sounds rather complicated,' Kate said. 'I'd better let you get on with it.'

Colin had decided to delve into a fictionalised version of Tina's past. Colin had many happy memories of the sweltering summer of 1976, and although Tina would have been a little younger than himself at that time, it would no doubt be a summer that would be etched into her mind.

With Tina being such a charitable person, Colin decided her character should be rewarded for such kindness. He didn't always change names of the characters he'd come across in real life, but in this case he wanted her story to have the best chance possible of coming true. And experience told him that success lay in his use of anagram when choosing a name for his character. Colin decided to call Tina, Nita.

He was pondering how Nita could be rewarded, when in walked Tilly with another woman. Tilly was the woman who'd stuck up for him when Blake almost pushed him over whilst waiting in the queue at the sandwich bar. Since then, they often spoke as they waited in the queue, and Colin came to learn that Tilly worked at the letting and estate agents in the city centre.

'Hi,' she said, as she waved over to him. The coffee shop was starting to get busy and tables were filling up. Tilly's eyes scanned the room for somewhere to sit.

'Hello,' he said. 'How lovely to see you here. You can have this table, if you like, I'm just leaving.' Seeing Tilly had given him an idea, and now he knew exactly how Tina – or Nita as she would be called – would be rewarded.

'Aw thanks,' Tilly said, as she joined Colin at his table. 'This is Nicole. My sister-in-law. I'm just showing her the place where I met and fell in love with her brother.'

'What in this very coffee shop?'

'Yes. Pretty much.'

'It doesn't surprise me,' Nicole said. 'This place does have a certain magic about it.'

'See, Bristol is an amazing city. There's nothing for you to worry about at all.' Tilly turned her attention away from Nicole to address Colin. 'Nicole's son is coming to university here next week. She's worried about him being in a strange place on his own.'

'I know, I'm being silly,' Nicole said. 'But you don't stop worrying about your children just because they're grown-ups.'

As Colin walked away, not only did he have Tina's story mapped out, but he had another two stories lined up…

Tina (Nita)

The Ladybird Witch

I stand outside the two-up, two-down, terraced house. Its 1980s nosey-net style curtains and bright-red door adorned with black knocker and letterbox look back at me. Being halfway between my elderly parents' house in one direction, and halfway to the animal rescue centre, where I work, in the other, I couldn't have chosen anything more perfect if I'd picked it myself. I can't believe it's mine: who'd just give me a house? I've gone through a list of relatives but there's nobody I can think of. Whoever it is, after the run of bad luck I've had lately, I'm very grateful.

Last week, my landlord told me he was selling up and I needed to move out. With my colleague, Kirsty, offering to cover for the afternoon, I visited the letting agent.

The saleswoman, Tilly, was really friendly. She showed me everything she had on the books, but everything was out of my price range. It was completely hopeless. It looked like I'd be sharing a bed with the last of the orphaned puppies that were brought into the centre a few weeks ago; unless a miracle happened.

On my way back to the bus stop, feeling completely miserable, I was standing at the lights waiting to cross the road. My mind was all over the place. I wasn't paying attention and stepped into the road whilst the lights were still green. A double-decker bus narrowly missed me. If it wasn't for the person standing behind me, who yanked me back onto the pavement, I wouldn't be here now. I turned to thank the stranger who saved my life, but nobody was behind me. Another pedestrian pointed out a woman with dark hair wearing a red dress who'd already fled.

When I arrived home that night, there was an envelope sitting on the doormat. It had been hand-delivered and looked official. After receiving the eviction notice, my stomach twisted. Part of me didn't want to open it. I put it on the side table in the hall, deciding to open it later. Or perhaps the next day. I made a cup of tea. Put a jacket potato in the microwave. Unloaded the washer drier. The microwave pinged; I was about to eat dinner, but my stomach was still churning. Not knowing what was in the letter was eating me up inside. I knew I had to face things.

Taking a deep breath, I ripped open the envelope. It was the best way, like peeling off a plaster. There were two letters inside. The first was from Tilly at the letting agent, explaining that after I'd called in that afternoon, there had been another visitor to their offices. The second letter enclosed was from that person's solicitor. I had to read it twice. The letter informed me I was now the owner of the most perfect two-bedroomed terraced house that I'd been looking at in the estate agent's window earlier. Tilly had asked if I wanted to view it, but I'd told her I was looking for a rental property and buying a place of my own was out of the question. I thought the letter was a prank at first, so the next day I visited Tilly at the letting agent. I expected her to laugh at me, but she confirmed everything was legitimate. The only thing she couldn't tell me was who my mystery benefactor was. The only clue was that it was a woman who was just a few years older than myself. So, it wasn't an elderly aunt or uncle. Tilly's lips were sealed, but she promised me that all would be revealed in good time.

I reach inside my bag and check the time on my phone. It will be another fifteen minutes before I'm due to meet my fairy godmother. The midday sun penetrates my bare neck and arms as I remove my sunglasses and wipe away the pool of perspiration nestled between my brows. A low stone wall encases the garden of my new home. A cherry tree hangs down, shielding the wall from the piercing sun like a Japanese parasol. I walk over and sit down; the shade instantly cooling my burning skin. The sound of birdsong loosens the knot in my shoulders, as I lean back against the tree and relish the warm breeze filtering through the umbrella of cherry blossom. The owner of a bicycle pings their bell as something tickles my arm; it's a ladybird, reminding me of another hot day many years ago....

It was 1976, the hottest summer on record. Britain had not long voted to remain part of the EEC, and ladybirds swarmed the nation. More importantly, it was the year I left primary school and had my first bicycle. I was coming up to twelve years old and considered myself virtually a grown-up.

My best friend, Heidi, who'd always lived in the

house next door moved away to a village on the outskirts of town. There was no more somersaulting over our orange space-hoppers, no more building dens in the abandoned allotment plots at the back of our house, and no more going to Brownies together. My life was over as I knew it. Until, in an attempt to compensate for losing my best friend, my parents bought me a bicycle. My passage to freedom. If Heidi couldn't come to me, then me and my bicycle would just have to go to Heidi.

There was one obstacle in my way. I'd only been to Heidi's new home, an old cottage with a thatched roof, once before. I was with Heidi and her mother then, so there was no chance of getting lost. It was about four-and-a-half miles away - across the dual carriageway, under the railway bridge, past the stream, past the church, and through to the other side of the village. There was no way my parents would let me cycle there on my own; especially since I didn't know where I was going. But what they didn't know wouldn't hurt them.

As soon as my parents left for work, I ran to the telephone table in the hall and picked up my mother's book that contained all her telephone numbers. It looked like a mini telephone, and you dialled the letter of the person whose number you wanted.

Heidi's surname was Peters, so I dialled 'P' and the book sprung open. I picked up the chunky receiver of the red telephone and dialled Heidi's number.

'Hello,' a familiar voice echoed down the line.

'Heidi, is that you?'

'Yes. Yes, it is. Nita? Is that you?'

'How did you guess?' It had been almost three weeks since Heidi and I had last seen each other, and my heart rate settled down as I discovered that she hadn't forgotten me.

'I'd know your voice anywhere, silly.' Heidi said. 'I can't believe I'm actually speaking to you. How are you?'

'Well, it's boring here without you. But guess what?'

'Tell me, tell me. What is it?'

'I have a new bike. Mum and Dad are at work so I'm going to cycle over to your house.'

'Nita, that would be fantastic. But how do you know how to get here?'

'I'll find it. It can't be that difficult. I know as far as the stream, I think.'

'Well, I could come and meet you by the stream with Nancy; she's almost fourteen, so she'll know how to get there.'

'Okay. Who's Nancy?'

'Nancy lives nearby. My mother has become friends with her mother, so we've kind of got stuck together.'

'Is she nice?' I imagined a grown-up girl who was pretty and clever. She would have lots of friends and all of them would want to be her best friend, but she would choose Heidi. And then Heidi would forget all about me. A picture of Heidi and Nancy having sleepovers, staying awake until midnight, sharing stories and sweets, formed in my head.

'She's okay. Not as much fun as you though.'

The knot in my stomach loosened as I discovered Heidi still considered me to be her best friend. It intrigued me what Nancy was like, and I arranged to meet them both at the stream. I took my packed lunch out of the fridge and put it in a cool bag together with an ice pack and a bottle of orange squash. I went over to the blue kitchen dresser where my mother kept a notebook and pen for her shopping list and pulled down the hatch. I couldn't tell her where I was really going, so I left a note pretending I'd gone swimming at the new sports centre at the top of the road. I was a strong swimmer, so she wouldn't mind me doing that. I was just about to click the hatch back into place when I noticed a bar of chocolate hidden at the back. I thought this would go down

nicely with my sandwiches, so added that to the bag
as well.

I put my bag of goodies into the basket at the
front of my bicycle and set off down the road. I was
shaky on my two wheels at first, but soon got the
hang of it. There was an underpass that went
underneath the dual carriageway to the other side of
the road, so I headed in that direction. The heat of the
sun scorched my arms as I held onto the handlebars.
A bead of perspiration formed on the top of my lip
and the plastic saddle was becoming slippery, as if
the heat had made that melt too. When I reached the
underpass, the coolness of the tunnel provided a brief
respite from the blistering heat. I was feeling thirsty,
and the thought of the delicious chocolate made my
tummy grumble. I was about to stop for refreshments,
but the roar of traffic overhead made me cycle
through to the other side as fast as I could. I imagined
my parents coming home from work and wondering
where I was before a policeman came knocking at the
door to say I'd been buried alive under a volcano of
melted tarmac.

My next stop would be the railway bridge. I was
a little unsure which way to head, but then I heard a
train rumbling past in the distance, so followed the
sound. After a while, I spotted the bridge ahead of me

and let out a sigh of relief as I discovered I was going in the right direction. I cycled on, feeling pleased I'd travelled such a long way all on my own.

Just after I passed the railway bridge, the road forked in two. I couldn't remember seeing this when I came here before and didn't know which road to choose. A ladybird flew down and landed on my handlebars before flying off down the road that forked to the left. There were a lot of ladybirds around that summer and my father said they were lucky, so I considered this to be a good sign and followed the same path as the ladybird. The path sloped upwards, and I pedalled harder. Unlike the roar of the underpass, the pathway was peaceful. I could hear the trickle of the stream and realised I was on a bridge with the stream flowing beneath me. There hadn't been a bridge last time I was here. Had I taken the wrong turn? So much for ladybirds being good luck. I was just about to turn back the way I came when some boys ran past, almost knocking me off my bicycle.

'Hey look where you're going,' I called after them. But they just laughed.

'Get off and milk it,' one of them shouted.

'Wow, you're original,' I called back, but they'd already gone.

It was then I first heard it. Only a faint whimper at first. Then a bit louder, and a splashing sound followed by a bark. I looked over the side of the bridge but couldn't see anything. There were steps heading down towards the stream where the boys had come from, so I jumped off my bicycle and bumped it down the steps. The sound was coming from under the bridge. I dumped my bike down on the grassy bank, pulled off my sandals, and rolled up my jeans. Holding on to the bridge wall for support, I made my way down the bank and peered under the bridge. Right in the centre of the stream was a small golden coloured dog, splashing around. It looked as if it could swim, but the water looked deep and the current was taking it downstream. I needed to do something fast.

I ran around to the other side of the bridge and looked to see if there was a stick or something else I could use to entice the dog back to the bank. But there was nothing. It looked like I would go swimming after all. The water came almost up to my chest, its coolness refreshing my burning skin as I waded through. Although I'd passed my bronze award at the swimming club, this was different; there was no force of the current at the swimming pool. It crossed my mind there was nobody else around if I drowned, but

I pushed this to one side and focussed on grabbing the dog. I'd entered the water a little further downstream from the dog, so by the time I reached the centre, I was in touching distance. Momentarily, I thought about what I'd do if it bit me? But there was no time to consider something that might not happen; I had a job to do. I held out my arms, and the puppy paddled into me, whimpering and licking my face. I needn't have worried about him not being friendly. I waded back to the bank and the puppy, who I could now see was a male golden retriever, clung on to me; his paws clutching my neck and his head on my chest like a baby.

When we reached the bank, I needed something to stop him from running off again, so I took the belt from my jeans and looped it through his collar. I grabbed my sandals and climbed to the top of the bank. Now I could see the wrong turning I took ran parallel to the road I should have taken; the stream ran between them. If I stayed walking along the edge of the bank, I would eventually come to the place where I was meeting Heidi.

As I made my way to our meeting place, I saw two girls. One lay on the grass and the other was shouting. As I got closer, I could see the girl shouting was Heidi and she was calling for help. The other girl, who had long dark hair, looked like she might be dead. The puppy pulled towards them, and it was hard to keep up with him and steer my bike at the same time.

Heidi came running towards me. 'Nita, I'm so glad to see you. And Wallis: you've rescued him.'

'Oh my God, what's happened?' I looked at the girl laying on the grass.

'It's Nancy. She has this disease where she needs to eat chocolate. I mean like, she has to have it, or she could die.'

I thought of the chocolate in my bag and knew how she felt. 'So, she's not dead yet then?'

'No.' Heidi looked at me horrified, as if saying such a thing might make it true. 'She became dizzy and took out her chocolate to eat it, then these horrid boys came along and snatched it from her, then Wallis chased after them and before we knew it he'd jumped into the water, and then Nancy ran after him, and then she collapsed. Oh, Nita, it's so awful, I don't know what to do.'

'Well, we mustn't panic. Remember what Brown Owl taught us. We must stay calm. And I have some chocolate, so I suppose she can have it.'

I took the chocolate out of my bag and pressed it against Nancy's lips. A ladybird crawled over her face and she woke up. She tried to raise her head and made a mumbling sound. I wondered if she was thirsty too, so took the orange squash out of my bag. Placing my hand at the back of her head, I gently raised her a little before tipping juice into her mouth. Nancy became more coherent and sat up. I gave her the rest of the chocolate bar.

'Thanks.' Nancy swept her long hair off her face, shaking her head so her hair fell down her back like a sheet of silk. 'You must be Nita; I've heard so much about you. And you've found Wallis.' Her mouth curled into a smile as Wallis jumped on her, licking her face.

When we returned to Heidi's house, Mrs Peters rang my mother at work to let her know where I was. It was agreed Heidi, Nancy and I would have a sleepover at Heidi's house. We stayed up until the early hours of the morning, sharing eerie tales. What Heidi hadn't mentioned before was that Nancy didn't just live nearby, but her father owned the Manor House. Heidi's new cottage was within the walls of the original estate. Mrs Peters wasn't exactly friends with Nancy's mother – she was her housekeeper.

'Have you lived here a long time?' I asked Nancy as we tucked into a big bowl of Golden Wonder crisps.

'I was born here,' she said. 'And my family have lived here for centuries. My ancestors didn't always live in the manor house, though. My great, great, and many other greats, Grandmother Agnes lived in this very cottage. I'm named after her. Nancy is a modern name for Agnes.'

'Hold on a minute. Don't tell her just yet,' Heidi said. 'Let me get us more drinks.'

Heidi returned with fresh glasses of dandelion and burdock, and Nancy continued with the tale of her ancestors.

'The old lady who used to live in the big house a very long time ago, I mean like hundreds of years ago - well, the villagers thought she was a witch. The only person who believed in her was Grandmother Agnes. She was her housekeeper and lived up in the big house with the old lady.'

The floorboard on the landing outside of Heidi's bedroom creaked. A shiver ran down my spine, but it was only Mrs Peters who'd come to check up on us. Once she'd gone, Nancy carried on with her story.

'One day, loads of angry villagers marched up to the house. A boy had been caught stealing apples from the orchard and a couple of days later he was found drowned in the stream. As you know, parts of it are deep. Everyone thought the old lady had put a curse on him, and they wanted to throw her in the stream, just like the boy. Grandmother Agnes tried to stop them. She said they were making a mistake, and the old lady had told the boy he was welcome to take as many apples as he wanted. But they didn't believe her.'

'That's terrible.' I looked over at Heidi and she moved closer to me and squeezed my hand. 'So, what happened?'

'They dragged the old lady to the stream, saying if she was a witch she'd float; and if she was innocent then she'd sink.'

'But that's silly.'

'I know, but it's what they did back in the seventeenth century.'

'We learned about it at school.' Heidi reminded me.

'So, did she drown?'

'Yes, and no. The villagers had all gone home, but Grandmother Agnes stayed behind. She was sitting by the stream crying when a ladybird landed on her arm. Grandmother Agnes loved ladybirds. She said wherever there was a ladybird there was hope. The ladybird flew off and landed on a lily pad floating on the water, before disappearing into the stream. Grandmother Agnes thought it was an omen.

She used to bathe in the stream when she was a young girl and knew the current well. She jumped in and pulled out the old lady's body. It turned out the old lady was a witch, after all. A nice one, though. She'd used her powers to pretend to drown but had become trapped and couldn't escape.'

'Your Grandmother Agnes saved her life?'

'She did, just like you saved mine today. And Wallis' too. Although Grandmother Agnes said it was the ladybird who was the real heroine. If it hadn't landed on her arm, she wouldn't have believed there was hope or had the courage to jump into the water.'

I told them about how I'd followed the ladybird and asked if they thought the ladybird had saved Wallis' life by making me go down the wrong road. Nancy said ladybirds were magical creatures, and some people in her village said they were reincarnations of the good witches who tried to cast good spells over the village. We all agreed the ladybird had changed our fate that day.

'But how did your ancestors come to live in the big house?'

'Grandmother Agnes was a heroine after that day. When the old lady didn't float, the villagers felt terrible. And later a man admitted he'd seen the boy messing around near the water. The old lady had no children and when she died, many years later, she left the manor house to Grandmother Agnes in her will.'

'Wow. Grandmother Agnes sounds incredible.'

'She was. But that's not all. Since that day, the village has another folklore where if somebody saves your life then you have to always look out for them, or you'll die as if they hadn't rescued you at all. The spell is only broken if you save their life in return. And if you do, you still have to give them the one thing they desire the most.'

A car door slams, bringing me back to the present moment. A woman with dark hair cut into a stylish bob, wearing a red dress and dark sunglasses, walks over. There's something familiar about her, but I can't quite make it out. But as soon as she speaks I recognise her. The way her mouth curls up into a smile.

'Hello,' she says, lifting her dark glasses off her face. 'You must be Nita.'

Tilly

Stranger on the Train

It's funny how a kettle distorts your reflection. My face looks longer; not so fat. My nose and mouth as if they don't belong to me. My eyes are the only feature I recognise as being mine. I never liked my eyes when I was younger. I always wanted blue eyes like my best friend, not green eyes like my mother. Ironically, now my mother is dead, I relish any similarity I have to her. Ever since I was a child, there was nothing I couldn't do in my mother's eyes. When I struggled with my keywords in the reception class, she made funny sentences so I remembered them. When my recorder phase made her ears bleed, she told me that practice made perfect. When I made mistakes, she told me mistakes were good because they made us do things better next time. When all else failed, she made tea.

As the kettle boils, my hand reaches down to my tummy as I feel my unborn daughter kick. With my other hand, I pour boiling water into my *Twirl* mug. Like my eyes, the mug bought by my mother last Easter has become more precious.

I carry my tea over to the small table overlooking the garden. The apple blossom is trying its utmost to make an appearance and the golden daffodils are in full bloom, reminding me of the vibrant yellow sunflowers that were growing in Nicole's garden the day I found out I was pregnant.

I met Nicole six months ago, through my job as an estate agent. I usually worked in the Bristol office but was working in the Bath branch that day. At forty-three years of age, Nicole was only five years older than myself, but whilst I was still waiting for my Mr Right, she'd been married for almost twenty years. She already had two children, a boy aged fifteen, and a girl aged nine; but just when she thought her child-bearing days were a thing of the past, she unexpectedly discovered she was pregnant for the third time. Her small three-bedroomed terrace wasn't big enough for a family of five, and she'd put an offer in on a four-bed townhouse.

'Do you believe in reincarnation?' she asked after she'd thrown up when I was showing a client around her home. 'It's funny how birth follows death.'

Nicole hadn't long lost her father. The commonality of grief perhaps another reason we seemed to get on so well. Until then, I'd always thought morning sickness happened in the morning and put my own evening sickness, and tendency to cry at the least thing, down to the trauma of losing my mother. I thought my swollen and aching breasts were down to my late period; I never had been that regular. But the waft of Nicole's coffee, designed to entice prospective buyers, induced an early bout of evening sickness. Being on her third pregnancy, there was no fooling Nicole. She made our excuses and told the viewer we'd be in touch. After witnessing not one but two women throwing up in his prospective bathroom, I don't think he was interested anyway.

'I have a spare test somewhere,' she said, just as her phone rang. 'Hold on; let me just get this, then I'll fetch it for you.'

Nicole's face lit up as she answered the phone. I could tell the call was important and got up to leave.

'Oh, Lee, I'm in the middle of something important.' She raised her hand in the air, halting me to stay exactly where I was. 'Do you mind if I call you later, darling?' Nicole ended her call.

As we waited for the result, we sat in the garden, soaking up the late afternoon sun, whilst I told her all about the stranger I'd met on the train on the way back to Bristol following my mother's funeral.

The tube was even more packed than usual that Friday morning. I found a pole to cling to but couldn't help avoiding eye contact with the stranger sharing the same pole.

'Cheer up it might never happen,' he said.

'It already has,' I told him. I'd only buried my mother the day before.

'I'm so sorry, trust me to put my size twelves in it.'

I couldn't help but glance down at his feet.

He got off at Paddington, my stop. I couldn't see where he'd gone; his stride being much quicker than mine. The 09:30 London Paddington to Bristol Parkway arrived on time for a change, but filled with passengers quickly. I grabbed the first seat I came across and as I reached to take my book from my trolley case, I couldn't help but recognise the shoes of the man sitting next to me.

'We meet again. Oliver,' he said, holding out his hand.

'Tilly.' As I shook his hand, my tummy flipped

over.

The usually long and boring journey flew by. I apologised for snapping at him on the tube and told him about my mother and how lost I'd felt without her. He told me how he'd lost somebody close to him recently too. We were just going through Bath when he asked if I would join him for lunch when we reached Bristol. He knew a fabulous little coffee shop near to the hotel where he was staying and wanted to treat me for making his usually dull train journey so enjoyable.

The food at the coffee shop was delicious. Being a carb addict, I chose a crusty baguette. Oliver had a salad. I decided on lemon tart for dessert. Oliver said he was full. I told him he was a spoilsport and didn't want to eat on my own. We compromised by asking for two forks so we could share. It was to die for. One of the best lemon tarts I've ever tasted. But Oliver was chivalrous, pretending to feign disinterest, allowing more for me. I felt bad about eating so much of it, so fed forkfuls into his mouth until he agreed how good it was. We stayed all afternoon until the five o'clock rush started, and the coffee shop filled up with workers dropping in on their way home.

'You don't fancy coming back to my hotel for a coffee, do you? No funny business, I promise.' He was lying, of course.

The sex was amazing. He was amazing. I can vouch for what they say about the size of men's feet.

'Bastard. How could he use you like that?' Nicole was angry on my behalf as I told her my story.

'It wasn't like that. He wanted to see me again, but I was the one who sneaked off.'

'So, what happened?' Nicole asked.

'As I said, he was so attentive. Not just in bed; he was interested in everything I had to say too. He even let me have the free chocolates the hotel left in his room. Then he started acting weird. He went to the bathroom but took his man-bag with him. He was gone for a while. I knocked on the door, but he didn't answer. There wasn't a lock on the door, so I opened it. I wanted to make sure he was okay. He had his back to me and didn't see me come in. I was about to say something when, through the reflection in the mirror, I saw him injecting himself with a needle. I freaked out, grabbed my things and made a run for it.'

Two blue lines appeared on the test.

'I can't possibly be pregnant. I'm on the pill.'

'Have you been ill recently or on anti-biotics?' Nicole asked.

'Yes. I had a chest infection.' My GP had told

me they'd reduce the effect of my contraceptive pill, but as I was virtually a virgin again I took little notice.

Being an expert on these matters, Nicole told me how many weeks pregnant I was, and worked out that we were due at roughly the same time.

Now, although I'm getting used to the idea that I'm going to be a single mother, I'm still nervous about my first antenatal class this evening. But like my mother always said, *tea solves everything.* I dunk the teabag several times and stir my drink, but as I fish it out I notice the bag has split, leaving a collection of leaves at the bottom of the amber liquid. My mother often read her tea leaves, and I can't help but think she's had a heavenly influence on this. Out of curiosity, I finish most of the tea, then dump the remnants onto a saucer before looking to see what *symbols* remain in my mug. Leaves around the rim represent the present: there's a bridge shape which means I'm undergoing a life-changing event or have met somebody who will change my life. I can't argue with that; pregnancy is a major life-changing event. Remnants around the middle of the cup represent the future: a heart - this means love, home, and romance. I already love my baby, and my home is my haven from the outside world. But as for romance, Oliver has put me off for the foreseeable future. Leaves at the bottom represent the answer to my problem: two tree-like shapes stand out, representing family unity. That's nonsense for a start. My father walked out when I was a child, and with no siblings, my family is just me and my unborn daughter. The thought scares me. How will I look after her on my own, with nobody to tell me if I'm doing things right or wrong? Nobody to share her first step, her first word.

At least I have Nicole. She's become like the sister I've never had and is coming along to antenatal class with me. Talking of which she should be here by now. I'm about to call her when I hear her car pull up outside.

'Sorry, Tills.' Nicole hugs me as soon as I open the door. 'Ollie just turned up on my doorstep.'

'Who's Ollie?' I ask as I grab my jacket and we make our way out to her car.

'My brother,' she says.

'I thought your brother was called Lee?' I remembered her phone call: *Oh Lee... I'm in the middle of something important.*

'No, it's definitely Ollie,' she laughs. 'Actually,' Nicole says in a voice that tells me she'd been up to something. 'I thought you might like to pop over for dinner tomorrow evening? I think you'd get on well with my brother.'

Nicole had been trying to matchmake for ages, but after what happened with the stranger on the train, I wasn't ready to let another man into my life.

'Ollie's a type-one diabetic. He's a bit of a party pooper when it comes to dessert, but he's a great guy. Good looking too.' This is him here,' she says, showing me the picture on her phone.

A stab of guilt hits me as I realise that I almost inadvertently killed this gorgeous man with lemon meringue pie. 'I think we're already acquainted,' I tell her.

~~~

Colin

The Story Collector – Part 3

Colin was standing in the queue at the sandwich bar. It was another sweltering day, and it reminded him of the time when Abby and Lucas had met. He'd often thought about the story he was going to write about Blake, but he just couldn't think of anything suitable. And with his characters all being linked in some way, finding a connection between his latest story and Blake was proving harder than anticipated.

Colin was pleased with how he'd been able to connect his characters. Abby knew Stella. Stella knew Emily. Emily's friend's sister lived next door to Paula. Paula knew Kirsty. Kirsty knew Tina. And when Colin saw Tilly in the coffee shop that day, he was reminded of how Tina had tagged herself at Tilly's letting agency when looking at a property. It turned out to have been snapped up before she managed to view it, but showed Tina was connected to Tilly. And now Tilly was connected to his latest story of Nicole.

Nicole's story was almost finished. He'd received feedback from his writing group, and it just needed a few final tweaks before it was published. But unless Colin could find a connection between Nicole and Blake – or Kaleb as he would be called in Colin's literary world - then it looked like the chain would be broken, and Blake would be getting away with his misdemeanours.

The sandwich bar was busier than ever, and Colin heard the girl behind the counter (whose nametag identified her as *Skye)* complaining how she hated working there. Skye was usually so cheerful, but today it seemed something, or somebody, had upset her.

'You're so lucky going off on maternity leave,' she said to her colleague.

'Yes, I suppose I am,' her colleague said. 'It's a shame you don't get paid to have babies, though. It's bloomin hard work being pregnant.'

Colin reached a moment of epiphany. He remembered what Kate had told him about using a surrogate. And she was always telling him how she'd love to be a character in one of his stories. What if Kaleb became embroiled in a blackmail plot surrounding surrogacy? But with his current story being about Nicole coming to terms with her son leaving home, how could he connect the two?

'Ah, now there's an idea,' Skye said to her colleague. 'Being paid to have a baby would be better than working here, that's for sure. At least I could keep up with my uni work, if I didn't have to spend half of my time, trying to make ends meet.'

Colin's interest was piqued. He hadn't realised Skye was a student as well. If he could connect Nicole's son to Skye through being at university together, then connect Skye to Blake through her job at the sandwich bar, she could prove to be the link between the two stories. But Skye seemed a nice girl; ideally, he wanted an extra link to come between her and Blake, rather than them being directly acquainted. Colin needed to do some thinking.

He crossed the road and sat down on a bench on College Green to eat his lunch. It was a great spot for people watching and ideas often came to him whilst sitting there. The cathedral clock was striking a quarter to the hour, but today Colin was in no rush to get back to work. The weather was far too nice to be stuck in the office all afternoon. Just as he finished his lunch, he heard shouting.

'I told you, I don't have your stupid phone.' A girl with red hair was screaming at Skye, as they made their way across the green.

'Yes, you do,' Skye said. 'You're the only one who had access to it, Alley. Who else could have taken it and sent him those messages? It certainly wasn't me.'

'You're such a paranoid bitch. I don't know what I ever saw in you.' The girl slapped Skye across the face, leaving her stunned.

Colin couldn't believe what he was seeing. It's no wonder poor Skye seemed upset earlier. He considered if he should check on her, see if there was anything he could do. He packed up his things and stood up to make his way towards her. But when he looked up, she was too far away for him to catch up with her.

Colin was about to leave when he noticed a young man with dark hair approach Alley. Blake? Colin had no idea whether Alley's name was spelt that way, of course. And he wasn't certain if the young man was Blake. But an idea was forming in his mind…

Nicole

Fortune Cookie

It's only been a short journey from our home in Bath to our son's new student accommodation in Bristol, where he will be living for at least the first year of his five-year medical degree. Fourteen miles door to door to be precise. I know I have to let Daniel, our eldest child, fly the nest, but it still feels like I'm about to have one of my arms chopped off. If things went wrong when he was little – a grazed knee, a spilt drink, or a falling out with a friend – I could put everything to rights with a kind word and a cuddle. He was my world, and I was his. My love for him unconditional. Always. Now as he is about to leave the sanctuary of home behind, butterflies dance around in my stomach. Not only because of the exciting journey my son has in front of him, but because my unfaltering maternal instinct to protect him, no matter his age, is being torn away.

'This is it, son.' My husband, Matthew, looks at Daniel in the car's rear-view mirror as Bessie, our sixteen-year-old Volvo, judders to a halt as we pull up outside the tower block.

Matthew's been full of stories of his own student life throughout our journey. Stories of getting drunk and rolling in at all hours of the morning. Throwing up in the gutter. Not making it home at all some nights. Stories I'd rather not know about.

'Sure is.' Daniel's eyes scan the outside of the building, taking in its proximity to Welsh Back, renowned for its array of pubs; some located in historical buildings, others on boats floating in the harbour.

Despite it being a Sunday, the place is busy, both with pedestrians and traffic on the nearby main road that crosses over Bristol Bridge, leading to the city centre. A ferry boat full of passengers chugs along the river tooting its horn.

'That's the one on the website we looked at,' I say. 'You know, the one that goes from the city centre right up to Temple Meads train station.'

I turn to face Daniel. His eyes are bright with curiosity. As well as the university's reputation as one of the best places in the country to study medicine, it was the city's vibrant and eclectic culture that helped Daniel to decide to study here. I realise how lucky I am that he's chosen a university that's not too far from home. A short car ride, or train journey away should he need me.

I draw my eyes to the nearby *Spar*. At least he'll have access to proper food. A group of students come out of the shop and walk over to the main entrance of the building, carrying their daily essentials: bread and milk, crisps and beer. I'm glad I packed a box of store-cupboard essentials. Dried pasta, tuna, chopped tomatoes, that sort of thing. Matthew thinks I'm being ridiculous. 'Stop fussing, Nico,' he'd said. 'He's more than capable of sorting himself out with what he needs.'

We get out of the car. Matthew opens the boot and passes the heavy rucksack to Daniel. Matthew takes the big suitcase, and I take the smaller one with wheels.

The main entrance opens into a communal lounge. It's pretty empty at the moment, with last year's students having moved on to new accommodation, and this year's still moving in. There are a couple of squishy sofas, but most of the seating is in the form of hard plastic chairs. A large-screen television is placed up high on the far wall.

The other end of the room has table games: pool, ping-pong, and one of those tables with little plastic footballers. It reminds me of a cross between a waiting room and a pub.

On the left-hand side is the concierge's office, which has a sliding window looking out onto the communal area. Matthew goes over and introduces us. Daniel stays back and waits for me to catch up with him.

'I'll be okay, you know, Mum.' He places his free arm around my shoulder. 'And I'll still come and see you all the time.'

'I know.' I bite back the growing lump in my throat as I place my head on his chest, taking in the fragrance of his freshly washed T-shirt mingled with the smell of him. My boy.

'Hurry up, you two,' Matthew dangles Daniel's new room key in the air. 'Let's get that kettle on, I'm parched.'

'I knew I'd forgotten something,' I say, letting go of the wheeled suitcase. 'Stay here, I won't be a moment.'

The *Spar* is only small but there are quite a few customers. There's an older gentleman buying cigarettes, and a woman who must be in her late thirties with a toddler in a pushchair, but the other customers appear to be students. I make my way over to the beverages section and pick up a box of teabags. We usually have *Twinings* breakfast tea at home, but they only have *Spar* brand here. I make a note to send some decent teabags to Daniel in the post, but these will have to do for now. I can't remember whether I packed biscuits. I was so wrapped up in trying to make sure the hamper contained proper meals, I'd forgotten the very thing we needed after our journey. The biscuits are in the same aisle as the teabags and there's quite a selection for such a small shop. I pick up a packet of fruit shortcakes, Matthew's favourite; and some custard creams, Daniel's favourite. I like Bourbons, so scan the shelves looking for them. I'm just about to give up when I spot a single packet on the bottom shelf, tucked away behind a packet of ginger nuts. I reach down to pick them up, when a girl with dark-blonde hair, about Daniel's age, reaches over at the same time.

'It's okay, you have them,' I say.

'No, no, you have them.' The girl has a Scottish burr to her voice. Not overly so but it's just detectable. Her green eyes have a kindness behind them.

'I'm fine,' I say, showing her the other two packets that I'm holding. 'I'm good with these.'

'Well, only if you're sure?'

'Positive,' I say.

The girl takes the Bourbons to the cash-till and as I queue behind her, I see the Japanese gentleman shopkeeper pass her something from under the counter. When it's my turn to be served, he asks if I'm interested in any of their special offers on display. I'm tempted by the big bar of Cadbury's Dairy Milk but know it's far too many points and I have my weekly Weight Watchers weigh-in tomorrow, so reluctantly decline. He places the teabags and biscuits into a brown paper bag, and like he'd done with the girl with green eyes, he reaches below the counter and puts something else into the bag.

'What's that?' I ask.

'Fortune cookie,' he says. 'One for you, and one for your son.'

'Oh, thank you,' I say. But it's not until I've left the shop that I wonder how he knew I had a son.

'There you are, Nico, love,' Matthew says, as I walk back into the communal lounge. 'I was just about to come and see where you'd got to. Daniel's gone on up, his apartment is on the fourth floor.' He nods towards the ceiling.

We step inside the stainless-steel lift and travel up to what will be our son's new home. It's eerily quiet except for the sound of the whirling lift shaft. It's clean enough but there's an underlying staleness. The lift comes to a halt and we get out. Each floor of the tower block is split into six separate apartments. Each has a kitchen, a bathroom, an additional toilet, a living area, and four bedrooms – one for each student.

'We're here,' Matthew calls as he knocks on the main door of the apartment, even though it has been left ajar for us.

We hear the familiar sound of Daniel's voice coming from the kitchen, together with laughter. Leaving the suitcases in the hall, we head towards it.

'Mum, Dad, this is Penny,' Daniel says. 'One of my new flatmates. We've been chatting on WhatsApp over the last few months.'

'Nice, to meet you.' Matthew shakes hands with Penny. 'All this technology stuff is great isn't it, being able to vet each other before you share a place. Didn't have any of that in my day, had to put up with all sorts.'

'God, Dad, you're so embarrassing,' Daniel says.

'Nice to meet you.' Penny shares a look with

Daniel that says *my parents are just the same*. 'And nice to meet you, too. Again.' Penny holds out her hand, but then changes her mind and hugs me. 'I've just made a pot of tea; I thought you'd need one after your journey. I have some nice Bourbon biscuits too if I can tempt you.'

'I'd like that,' I tell Penny as I take the teabags and the biscuits I'd bought out of the paper bag and place them onto the kitchen work surface. I put the paper bag containing the fortune cookies into my tote bag, deciding to keep them for our other two children when we get home. I feel guilty leaving them at home with my brother Ollie, and my sister-in-law, Tilly; but there wasn't any room in the car for them with all of Daniel's things.

'I was thinking we could go and get a bite to eat in one of the pubs in King Street, once we've had tea,' Matthew suggests. 'Never mind the biscuits, I'm starving. And we can't turn down the opportunity of a pint whilst we're here.' Matthew winks at me. King Street was one of the first places we went together when we first started going out.

We decide to have our meal in The Llandogger Trow. The place where we'd first met. Both of us on separate nights out, venturing into Bristol with our respective friends. Being here not only fills me with a sense of nostalgia, but with the building dating back to the seventeenth century, you can't help but feel old ghosts of the past mingling in with the atmosphere of the present. As we tuck into cheeseburger, and chips that have been served in miniature stainless steel pails that appear both rustic and posh at the same time, Matthew fills Daniel and Penny in on the pub's history.

'Legend has it that both Robinson Crusoe and Blackbeard drank in this pub,' he says.

'Robinson Crusoe is a fictional character, Dad,' Daniel says.

'That may be so,' Matthew taps his head as if he has insider knowledge, 'but he was based on a real-life sailor that Defoe met in this pub.'

'I didn't realise that,' Penny says. 'That's amazing, isn't it, Dan? We'll be able to bring our flatmates here and tell them all about it.' I notice how much attention they pay to each other as they speak, and they remind me of what Matthew and I were like at that age.

'And what about Blackbeard?' Daniel asks.

'Well, it's well-known that he used to drink here. Bristol was the centre of the pirating world back in the day.'

Penny's face turns pale as if something has spooked her.

'Are you okay, sweetheart?' I ask. She's a long way from her home in Scotland, and without her family around her, I can't help but feel protective towards her. I hope Matthew's tales haven't scared her.

'Yes. It's just that… well, the Japanese man in the shop gave me a fortune cookie earlier. It said *A black-bearded man from the past will unite you with a fair-haired man who is destined to be your future.'* Her eyes look towards Daniel's fair hair.

But any idea of there being any truth in the proverb is dashed as the barmaid comes over and clears away our plates. She has blonde hair with curls that settle on her shoulders, and her name badge tells us her name is *Skye.*

'Oh, I wouldn't take any notice of those, cookie things, Penny,' Skye says. 'That oriental guy gave me one of those too when I moved into student accommodation. It said I'd meet a woman with a strange proposition, but nothing like that has happened to me.'

'This is Skye,' Penny says to Daniel. 'Skye's a third-year and is on the student union. I met her at Open Day.'

'Hi.' Skye holds out her hand to Daniel. Nice to meet you. You'll probably see me around uni quite a bit.'

'He gave me some of those too,' I say after Skye has taken our plates away. I pick up my tote bag from the floor under the table and pull out the fortune cookies. 'I was going to take them home for the children, but the Japanese man said one was for me and one was for my son.' I pass one to Daniel. 'What if there's something in the prophecy? Maybe we should open them?'

I'm stuffed after the cheeseburger and chips, but you need to eat the cookie for the prophecy to come true. Daniel's always had a good appetite and has no trouble wolfing down his cookie.

'What does it say?' Penny asks him.

'It says *you will sit in the seat of a pirate.*'

'Oh my God, that is so spooky,' Penny says.

But I know my son and can tell when he's fibbing. 'You'll get used to his sense of humour,' I tell Penny. 'What does it really say, Dan?'

'Strings of the past will never be broken but true happiness is in front of you.'

I wonder whether he's making it up again, but as he hands me the slip of paper, I'm shocked to discover he's telling the truth. Although I guess a prophecy like that could relate to a lot of students starting out on their journey into adulthood and away from home for the first time. Perhaps the Japanese gentleman has made the cookies especially for them. But then he didn't know I was going to hand this exact one to Daniel. What if I'd chosen that one for myself? It wouldn't have made sense then.

Now it's my turn. The cookie is surprisingly delicious. It's light and crisp with a hint of ginger and sesame. I hope the Japanese gentleman doesn't hand these out to customers with a nut allergy. I carefully unwrap the small piece of paper inside and read it out.

'An old friend will let you down, but a lady in yellow will come to your rescue.'

'That sounds like a load of old codswallop,' Matthew says.

'It does, doesn't it?' I can't help but feel a bit disappointed at my prophecy. Still, I decide to text Tilly and check on the children just in case there's something in it. Although she's my sister-in-law, we were friends before then. I know she'd never intentionally let me down, but what if something has happened beyond her control? It's better to be safe than sorry. She texts back straight away, attaching a picture of her and the girls baking, and I feel a tug of guilt at doubting her because of a stupid fortune cookie.

The afternoon flies by, and after another cup of tea back at Daniel and Penny's accommodation, we eventually arrive back at the car.

Matthew turns the key in the ignition. Nothing.

'Come on, Bessie girl,' he says. 'You can't let me down, now.'

We both look at each other as we realise what he's said. He turns the key again. It must be a fluke, that's all. But after several more attempts, our trusty old car that we've had since Daniel wasn't much more than a toddler, seems to have given up.

'Looks like it's the train home, then,' Matthew says.

After the tow truck has towed Bessie away, we walk around the corner to Welsh Back and wait for the ferry boat to take us on the short journey to Temple Meads train station. Despite the drama of Bessie breaking down, it's been a wonderful day full of memories of the past and the excitement of new ones to come. Daniel seems to have settled in okay. I had no idea he'd already made new university friends through WhatsApp. And Matthew is right; I do need to let go and allow him to make his own mistakes.

However hard that might be.

A tooting horn lets us know our river taxi has arrived. A yellow ferry boat with its name painted on the side: *Lady*.

~~~

Kate

The Surrogate

I place the last carefully counted batch of the ten-thousand pounds, bound with strips of white paper, into the backpack. It takes up such a small amount of space, contradicting the value of what it will be exchanged for. The legitimate 'expenses' have been electronically transferred but now she's threatening to keep her; to divulge our secret unless she receives more. There is no choice; nothing I wouldn't do to ensure she's mine. The thought scares me as I realise how true that is.

A rare inherited heart condition that stole the life of my mother during childbirth meant I'd long since resigned myself to the fact I'd never carry a child of my own. My career as an economics lecturer keeping me busy over the years. Friends and colleagues feigning jealousy of my independence; at being able to sleep for a solid eight hours or take a romantic weekend away at a moment's notice. But they couldn't hide the pity they really felt. I was the cliché 'always the godmother never the mother'. But as much as I adored my godchildren, it wasn't quite the same; and independence was no compensation for the void that could only be filled by motherhood.

It was the birth of my nephew that first gave me the idea. My sister had given birth to the most perfect baby boy who was the image of my brother-in-law; the same shape nose, the same eyes. 'There's no doubt who his father is,' people would say. I knew my husband, Tom, had accepted our fate at not being able to have children before he asked me to marry him, but seeing him holding our newborn nephew seemed so unfair. I was the one who couldn't bear a child, and my health condition meant adoption was complicated. The stress of the process alone could kill me. But there was no reason Tom couldn't be a father. All I needed to do was find the ideal surrogate.

I'd seen her around campus but hadn't taught her before this academic year. She wore her blonde hair the same as I did at her age; casually swept off her face with loose curls sitting on her shoulders. Her eyes the same shade of bluey-green as Tom's. She couldn't have been a more perfect fit. I learned that her name was Skye, and as the weeks went by, I realised she was different from the other economics students I taught. Most of them wore a serious look on their face as they scribbled handwritten notes into a notepad, soaking up every word of the lecture, but she casually took notes on her iPad. Rather than appreciating university life, her air of indifference told the world it was lucky she chose to be part of it. I overheard her telling one of the other students how much she hated her part-time job as a barmaid: how she wanted to find a different way to help fund her final year of university; something more unconventional. I knew I had to find the courage to approach her; pitch my proposal.

I waited outside her place of work, sitting in the car until she finished her shift. I felt like a stalker. I suppose I was. But it was a better alternative than approaching her on campus. At least in the outside world we were on equal terms. Two independent women discussing a business proposition. She was at liberty to refuse. What could go wrong?

She took it all in her stride when I asked her.

'I'll think about it and get back to you,' she said, like I was asking her to meet up for lunch rather than impregnate herself with my husband's sperm.

It was just two days before she came back to me with her answer.

'If I agree then I'll expect top marks in my assignments this year.'

A shiver ran through me as the enormity of what I was about to embark on sank in. The dream of becoming a mother a step closer, but it could mean the death of my career if anybody discovered our arrangement. I was surrounded by women who had it all. Colleagues. Old school friends. My sister. Women who had the privilege of choice. There had been no choice for me. Not where motherhood was concerned. But thanks to Skye that was about to change.

Tom pulls up the zip on the rucksack. 'I'll be as quick as I can,' he says as he offers me a perfunctory peck on the lips before lifting the bag from the kitchen table.

'I still think I should come with you,' I say.

'No. It's best this way, Kate. We can't risk anybody seeing the two of you together again.'

He's referring to the twelve-week scan. Skye wanted to go alone, but I insisted we went along, too. It was okay for her; the changes in her body as the pregnancy developed were a constant reminder of our child's existence. We weren't part of that. We needed to see him or her for ourselves; albeit a monochrome version. Skye reluctantly agreed, but insisted she made her own way there, despite her apartment being on our route.

The ante-natal clinic was part of the local hospital. A recent addition to the main Victorian building. Parking spaces were sparse, but we found one after circling the car park a couple of times. We'd arrived a little early, so I decided to freshen up whilst Tom found us seats in the busy waiting room. As I entered the toilets, I was startled to see Skye leaning against one of the washbasins, tapping away on her phone. She was supposed to keep a full bladder, and I was about to ask her what she was doing there when a young woman with bright red hair came out from one of the toilets. I felt a bead of sweat trickle between my breasts as we recognised each other. It was Leyla, an administrator at the university. I noticed her eyes glance towards Skye. Did I sense recognition? But she quickly turned her attention back to me as we acknowledged each other.

'Do you think she recognised you,' I asked once Leyla had left.

'Who?'

'The woman who just spoke to me. Who do you think?' Skye's nonchalance was starting to grate. Surrogacy wasn't illegal, but the way I'd gone about it wasn't ethical. If anybody at the university found out what I was doing, my position would be untenable. But if Skye hadn't recognised Leyla, then perhaps Leyla hadn't recognised her either.

The scan was the most beautiful thing I'd ever experienced. Not only did we get to see our child for the first time, but we also heard the tiny heartbeat. The scan also identified Skye was four weeks further along than we first thought. The midwife informed us this wasn't unusual. Apparently, as the fertilised egg implants into the womb this can induce a small bleed that is often mistaken for a light period, and cause confusion with dates. This news meant our child was conceived at the very first attempt of insemination. The second batch of Tom's sperm surplus to requirements.

I put the liaison with Leyla to the back of my mind and marked off the weeks on the calendar as our child grew and developed. Everything was going as planned until several weeks later when I was sitting in the university's café marking assignments.

'Hi, Professor Smyth. How's your daughter?' It was Leyla. She pulled out a chair and sat down.

137

'My daughter?' My hand shook as I placed my cup down onto the table in front of me and splashes of tea spilt onto the saucer. We'd recently discovered Skye was carrying a little girl. I'd already pictured her, and it felt like Leyla could see straight into my mind.

'Sorry. I just assumed the girl you were with at the ante-natal clinic was your daughter. Unless it's you that's pregnant? I guess women have their children when they're much older these days. I didn't mean to pry.'

'Yes, it was my daughter.' I couldn't help feel a little insulted that Leyla considered I was too old to be pregnant myself. At forty-one years of age, plenty of women had children at my age. Relief washed over me as I realised she hadn't recognised the surrogate as one of the students, but it scared me as to how easily the lie to her identity tripped off my tongue.

'How far along is she?'

'Twenty-one weeks,' I said. This time it wasn't a lie. The fact she meant the surrogate, and I meant my daughter that was growing inside of her, were just pedantics. 'What about you?'

'I lost my baby,' she said.

'Oh, I'm so sorry. I didn't know.'

'It's been hard coming to terms with things, but I'm getting there. Me and my partner hope to have another child soon. I'd love to have a daughter like you have. Your daughter looks just like you.'

'Do you think so?' It was reassuring to know I'd chosen well. If other people thought Skye looked like me then hopefully her biological daughter would look like me too.

'She's more like her dad though.' Leyla fiddled with the thumb ring on her right hand, and I noticed a slight flush on her neck.

'You have a good memory.' She'd only met Tom once, at the Christmas ball the year before last.

'I thought I recognised your daughter from somewhere, then realised she works at one of the pubs in town. Your husband was there last week, standing at the bar talking to her, then she took her break to sit at one of the tables with him. The way they paid attention to each other and laughed at each other's jokes. I wish I got on with my parents like that. You're really lucky.'

'When was this?' I'd met up with Skye several times since she'd become pregnant; making sure she had everything she needed. Showing her how to achieve top marks in her assignments. But I didn't know Tom had been seeing her as well.

'Um, Friday, I think. Yes, it must have been because I looked to see if you were there too before remembering it was the day you were away at the economics conference.'

'Oh, yes. Of course. I remember now.' What I really wanted to ask was whether she was sure it was definitely him, but I wasn't about to let my home life become the topic of office gossip. 'Actually Leyla, you haven't said anything about seeing me and my daughter at the clinic, have you?'

'No. Why?'

'It's just that my daughter is having a few problems with her pregnancy. I'd rather keep it quiet until we know everything is going to be okay.' It felt wrong making up such an excuse, especially with Leyla having lost her baby; but I couldn't risk any prying questions.

'Okay. If that's what you want. Your secret is safe with me,' she said.

After Leyla enlightened me as to Tom's whereabouts that Friday evening, I questioned him, feigning interest in the work he did as a local councillor. Did he take a client out for drinks? If the answer was 'yes' it might account for him being in the pub. An opportunity for him to say 'Yes, and by the way, I bumped into the surrogate.' But he didn't.

He gave nothing away to suggest he'd been anywhere near the place where Leyla had seen him. I wanted to believe him. He'd never given any reason for me to suspect he would cheat on me, but Skye was carrying his child. The one thing I couldn't give him.

As the pregnancy progressed, I had regular lunch dates with our surrogate. The thrill of being so close to my unborn daughter, yet so far, was almost unbearable. There were other updates too: videos of Skye's tummy as our daughter moved, little bumps poking and kicking like an alien trying to escape. I thought about asking whether she'd met Tom without me knowing about it, but everything was going as planned and I didn't want to risk rocking the boat.

A few weeks before our daughter was born, I was shopping at The Mall. Next Baby had an offer on, and I couldn't resist a final splurge before she arrived. I'd just placed a gorgeous little pink dress with matching socks and bonnet in my basket when there was a tap on my shoulder. It was Leyla.

'Hello, Professor Smyth. What a lovely dress.' She took it out of my basket to admire. 'I'd love this for my little girl.'

'Leyla. That's fantastic news. When are you due? And there's no need to call me Professor Smyth, just call me Kate.'

'I'm not pregnant. My partner is. She's due in a couple of weeks.' Leyla doesn't acknowledge that I've asked her to use my first name.

'So, your partner must have become pregnant before you?' I knew Leyla had been due to give birth about a month after Skye, so it didn't take much working out. I'd also assumed she'd conceived naturally; that her partner was a man. I guess the turkey-baster method was more popular than I'd realised.

'We didn't know she was going to keep the baby when I got pregnant. It was going to live with the biological father but that's not happening now.' Leyla put the dress back on the rack.

'Well, I'm glad things have worked out for you, anyway.' I lifted the dress off the rack and put it back in my basket.

'It's because he's a cheat. The father. His poor wife is so trusting. You can't stay with a liar, can you?' The way her eyes fixated on me as she spoke was a little too close for comfort, and I noticed the same flush on her neck that she had when she spoke to me in the university's café.

'I guess not. I'm lucky to haven't experienced anything like that.'

'Haven't you? How can you be so sure?'

'I'm sorry Leyla. What are you getting at?'

'Don't take any notice of me. I'm sure your husband adores you. And that pregnant daughter of yours. After all, you're going to be grandparents soon. Look, forget I said anything. I must get going. Nice to have seen you.'

I knew Leyla was judging by her own experience. After all, she knew nothing about me or Tom. How could she? But what she said had spoiled my afternoon. Was it really Tom that she saw that evening in the pub, talking to Skye? And did she see something going on between them that made her question how they knew each other?

As I arrived home, I heard Tom's raised voice as he spoke on the telephone.

'You stay away from her. I've told you, there is no more. You know as well as I do the photos don't give an accurate picture.'

'What's going on?' I ask.

'Darling. What are you doing home?' He abruptly ended the call.

'I've got a migraine coming on. Never mind that. Who were you talking to?'

'Oh, it's nothing. Just a council thing.'

'Really? It sounded heated.'

'They needed putting in their place but it's nothing to worry about; something and nothing.'

I'd planned on questioning him on whether he'd met the surrogate without me knowing about it. And now this; I could see the phone call had unsettled him, and what he said made little sense. But my migraine was kicking in, and my vision was starting to blur. I craved the sanctuary of a cool, dark room. I'd have to save my interrogation for another time.

I was in the middle of a lecture when our daughter was born. Skye sent a picture of her under a fluorescent lamp, as she was a little jaundiced. *Just catching some sun* the caption said. My nephew was jaundiced at birth too, and common sense told me it wasn't anything to be concerned about. But I couldn't help worry, as the intensity of needing to be with her burned through me. Being jaundiced didn't detract from the fact she was the most beautiful baby I'd ever seen. I couldn't wait to hold her in my arms, but Tom and I were on strict instructions to stay away from the hospital. Skye would contact us once she was home. With our daughter being jaundiced that meant it would be a little longer than we'd anticipated but she'd arrived safely and that was all that mattered.

I tried to focus on the class in front of me, but my mind was elsewhere. I had to pinch myself to believe the fact our daughter was finally here. A second text arrived from Tom. *Congratulations Mummy.* To say I was on cloud nine was an understatement. Events of the past few weeks had filled me with doubt as to my relationship with my husband. The conversations with Leyla, and the strange telephone call. But now I was sure he loved me just as much as I loved him.

I was wrapping up the lecture when another text arrived from Skye: *If you still want to go ahead and keep your secret safe it will be an extra 10k.* My heart was pounding and I couldn't think straight. The deal had been delivered, literally, but now she wanted more.

'Are you alright, Professor Smyth?' one of the students asked. My words had dried up. The air-conditioned lecture theatre felt hot and the students in front of me merged into one as my legs buckled beneath me.

'Sorry, I'm not feeling too good.' I held onto the desk in front of me, stopping myself from collapsing in a heap before escaping to the nearest toilets. I made it just in time before throwing up. After rinsing my mouth and splashing my face with cold water, I rang Tom. He answered straight away.

'I'm so sorry Kate, it's not what it seems,' he said. 'I've told her, there is no more.'

'What do you mean, Tom, it's not what it seems? And why did you tell her we can't pay? I'm not giving up now.' My heart was still racing, another clutch of nausea burned at the back of my throat, threatening to escape. All I could think of was how we were going to find the money.

'What did your text say?' He sounded scared as well as angry.

'The same as yours I imagine, that if we want to keep our secret safe then it will cost us another ten thousand pounds.'

'And there was no picture?'

'The photo of the baby came through just before. But you know that.'

'And that was the only photo?'

'Yes. Why did you get another one?' My reflection in the mirror was coming in and out of focus. Why was he asking stupid questions?

'Umm, no. Just the same as you, a threat asking for more money.'

'I don't care what it takes, we have to find the money.' There was no way I was going to let my daughter slip from my grasp.

'We're already mortgaged to the hilt. The bank won't let us have any more,' he said.

'It won't hurt to ask.'

'They won't. Trust me.'

'Then, I'll ask my sister.'

'Do you think she'll lend it to us?'

'I don't know but I have to try.' I said. 'It's our only hope.'

It wasn't until we finished the call that I wondered how he could be so sure the bank wouldn't lend us the money. Or when it was exactly that he'd informed the surrogate we weren't in a position to hand over more money. When the message came through, I'd rang him straight away. And his choice of words: *there is no more.* Where had I heard him say that before?

***

As soon as he drives off, my sister pulls up outside the house. It's a condition of her lending us the money that we follow him. When I asked her to lend us the money, the rollercoaster of emotions and insecurities of the last few months came flooding out. I told her about what Leyla had said, and the telephone call that day when I arrived home early; how I overheard him saying 'there is no more'. Tom wasn't one to bring problems at work home with him, but the call had left him more stressed than I'd ever seen him. Together with everything Leyla had inferred, I felt like I was becoming paranoid, but my sister assured me I had every right to be concerned. Everything seemed to point towards Tom and the surrogate running off into the sunset with our daughter and my sister's money, leaving me behind to pick up the pieces.

I jump in the passenger seat. It's a hot day; a band of sweat prickles at my top lip and between my eyebrows. I'm grateful for the cool respite of the car's air conditioning. As we pull out onto the main road, I can just about make out Tom's car ahead of us but there are several cars in between. We drive through town and past the university. Skye's apartment is the second turning on the right. I can't help but wonder how many times Tom's been there before? Just the two of them in their illicit love den. Has he felt our daughter's kicks as she moved around inside of her surrogate mother? I try not to think about it.

'It's this turning here,' I tell my sister.

'I didn't see him turn off, she says.'

'I can't see him ahead. And it's definitely this turning, so he must have.'

She flicks her indicator and turns right. Skye's apartment is about halfway up on the left-hand side, but I can't see Tom's car anywhere.

'Are you sure this is where they agreed to meet?'

I take out my phone and scroll through the messages. A catalogue of how my relationship with Skye grew before it was subsequently destroyed. Formal at first, then more friendly as we got to know each other. The last friendly message being the moment my daughter was born. I re-read the ones since then, double-checking the details of where and when we were to make our exchange. I hadn't noticed before but there's something both odd and familiar about the latest texts since the birth. I go back and read the earlier texts again. 'Hi Prof Smith,' progressing to 'Hi Kate.' And the later ones, 'Hello Professor Smyth.' The level of formality could be put down to the deterioration of our relationship, but it was the earlier more common but incorrect spelling of 'Smith' that stood out. Was it because she had finally worked out how to spell my name correctly, or was it something else?

'What is it?' my sister asks. 'Have we come to the wrong place?'

'I don't know… this is definitely where she lives but the text just says *3 o'clock - same place.* When the text came through I was in a panic, I read it as *my place*. What does she mean by *same place?* We don't have a usual meeting place in case anybody sees us together.'

'We're still early.' My sister checks the clock as she pulls up behind a parked car. 'Let's just see if she's at home before we work out our next move.'

We unfasten our seatbelts and get out of the car. It's a built-up residential area. The Victorian houses are huge and have mostly been converted into apartments. Skye's is on the first floor. I press the buzzer. We wait for what seems like several minutes, although in reality it's no doubt no more than a few seconds. When there's no answer, I press again. This time I hear a connection at the other end.

'It's me,' I speak into the intercom.

'Come on up.' She buzzes us in.

We mount the stairs. The door to the flat is ajar and we walk in to see her sitting in an armchair, feeding my daughter from a bottle. The ugly head of jealousy rips through me as I watch her cradling my baby in her arms.

'Where is he?' My sister rushes from room to room, opening doors.

'Who?'

'You know full well, who,' she says. It's like we're children again. With our mother dying in childbirth when I was born, my older sister has always looked out for me. Now she's taking charge once more.

There's no sign of him. But on the mantel is a picture of Skye with somebody I recognise. Leyla. They're standing next to each other, their heads leaning in towards each other as they pose for the camera.

'So you do know each other?' It was an obvious and stupid thing to say.

'I thought it was best if we kept life at the university out of all of this.' She removes the bottle from my daughter's mouth, lifting her into her own shoulder before gently tapping her back. 'I'm sorry I haven't contacted you, but I lost my phone. I had to wait until I came home from the hospital so I could get a new one and sync it with my computer, to access my stored numbers. I was going to ring you as soon as I could.' My daughter lets out a bubble of wind and undigested milk trickles onto the napkin placed over Skye's shoulder. 'There, that's better, isn't it little one?' She kisses my baby on top of the head before handing her to me as if it's the most natural thing in the world. 'It's time to meet your mummy.'

I feel my heart jump as if it's been dislodged from its normal place. I am intoxicated by her newborn smell. Her tiny mouth and nose. Her eyes are closed as she revels in a post-feed sleep. I'm jolted back to reality as I take in what Skye has just told me about her phone.

'What are you talking about? You messaged this morning after we arranged the cash from the bank. That's why I'm here.'

'I just thought you came around because you hadn't heard from me. What cash? The money has all gone through electronically.'

My sister looks at me puzzled, but I can see pieces of the jigsaw starting to fit together.

'How do I spell my surname?' I ask.

'What has that got to do with anything?'

'Just humour me.'

'S M I T H,' she spells out each letter.

I thought as much. Time hasn't accustomed her to the correct spelling of Smyth. But as the person responsible for HR functions of university staff, Leyla knows exactly how my name is spelt.

I walk over and show her the recent texts.

'I don't understand?' she says. 'I never sent those texts, I swear. And that one sent earlier today, well I was asleep then.' She points to the text that asks if we have the money yet. 'I'd been up since the early hours, and Leyla insisted I go and get some rest. You can ask her if you don't believe me. She should be back soon.'

'It's okay, I believe you, but I need to ask you something, and I need you to answer me honestly.' I'd put the question off for too long and now it was time I learned the truth. 'Have you ever met my husband at a time that I don't know about?'

'Only once.' She wraps her arms tightly around her body, reminding me of the way she's swaddled my daughter in the cool cotton sheet. 'Leyla's miscarriage left her in a bad way. Her head was all over the place. She started going on again about us keeping your baby.' Skye pulls a tissue from her sleeve and blows her nose. 'I would have done anything to make her happy, honest I would. But I couldn't go back on my word with you; it wasn't fair. Not until she told me about...' She raises her hand and rubs her forehead. 'Look, it was nothing. She'd got it all wrong.'

'She got what wrong?' My daughter gives a contented whimper and I pull her in closer, realising more than ever how lucky I am to have her in my arms.

'I'm sorry. I can't deal with this. You have your baby. It's probably best if you leave before Leyla returns.' Her eyes glance towards the window.

'I can't leave you on your own like this,' I tell her. 'You're obviously upset.' I hand my baby to my sister and steer Skye over to the sofa. I sit down next to her. 'If you tell me everything that's gone on, then maybe I can help you.' I'm aware the baby blues are playing a part in her emotional wellbeing, but I can't help but feel there's more to it. She usually appears so confident, but underneath the persona, she's just as vulnerable as any other young woman her age. I no longer see her as a threat, but an older version of my daughter that needs my help. 'You said Leyla wanted to keep the baby *again*. Tell me about how that started.'

'Before you made your offer, Leyla had been talking about us having a baby of our own. I wasn't keen. Not for a few years yet, anyway. I wanted to finish my degree, get my career off the ground, maybe pay off some of my student loan. Then you asked me to be your surrogate. It seemed the perfect

154

opportunity to help set us up for when we started a family. Leyla encouraged me to go ahead with it. But the moment I found out I was pregnant she changed her mind and wanted to keep the baby for ourselves. I told her I couldn't do that. She said I thought more of your feelings than hers and walked out on me.' Skye's bottom lip starts to quiver.

'I had no idea you'd been through any of this.' I tuck a strand of hair that's escaped back behind her ear, then take hold of her hand and return her gaze.

'She came back the next day, saying she'd come up with a solution. It was still early days for the pregnancy and at that point I still hadn't told you. She said if I was adamant about going through with the surrogacy then we should pretend the first try hadn't worked. That we should get another batch of sperm from your husband, for her to use. I didn't want her to leave me again so went along with it.'

'So Leyla's baby was Tom's?' My stomach turns over as I realise the consequences of what I've put my husband through.

'Yes.' A flush creeps into her cheeks. At least she has the decency to look ashamed of what she'd been part of.

'And you already knew you were further along than you'd told us when the scan confirmed the dates?'

'It was one of the reasons I wanted to go to the ante-natal clinic on my own. And because Leyla had her scan the same day. I didn't want you bumping into each other. It was a bit of a shock when you arrived early and came into the toilets. Leyla had just had her scan when we saw you.'

'And it was just after Leyla lost her baby, that you met up with Tom without me knowing about it?'

'Leyla heard a rumour that your husband was having an affair with one of the other councillors. I was angry. I thought you two were rock solid. I'd never have agreed to bring a child into this world otherwise. Leyla said the baby would be better off with us.'

'Why didn't you say anything to me?'

'I was going to. Remember when we met at that park, the one near the airport, with the ducks and the teashop?'

'I do. It was a lovely afternoon.'

'You were so kind to me. And so thoughtful bringing a picnic basket full of the things I like. I'd planned on talking to you about it then, but I just couldn't go through with it. What if Leyla was wrong? I didn't want to be responsible for splitting you up over something that was just a rumour. Then when you said you were going away on some conference. I decided it would be the perfect opportunity to speak to Tom about it instead.'

'How did he react?' My heart pounds as I await the answer. Leyla had opened up questions in my mind, but now I'm beginning to realise she had an ulterior motive.

'He seemed genuinely shocked at what I'd said. Completely denied there was any truth in it. Nobody can be one hundred per cent sure whether another person is telling the truth, can they? But I was as sure as I could be that Leyla had got it wrong. The surrogacy meant everything to him; the same as it did to you. I knew for certain he'd be a fantastic dad to your baby.'

'I know this is hard, sweetheart, but Leyla has been lying to both of us. When was the last time you can remember seeing your phone?'

'It was just after the baby was born. I sent you the photo of her in the incubator, and then Leyla took some more photos of us together.'

'And did she give the phone back to you?'

'She said she did, but I can't remember. The incubator was in the nursery. I'd lost quite a bit of blood and the midwife said I needed to go back to the ward and get some rest. Leyla went home. When she came back to the hospital later, I asked her about my phone but she said she gave it back to me. I asked the midwife if I'd left it in the nursery, but nothing had been handed in.'

'We need to ring Tom before he hands over the money. If it's not too late.' My sister places my daughter down in her Moses basket before taking her mobile out of her bag. The phone goes straight to voicemail.

'I've just had a thought,' I say to Skye. 'You said you couldn't ring me until you'd synced your new phone with the cloud.'

'Yes, that's right.'

'Do you back up your text messages on the cloud too?'

'Yes, I think so.'

'So, if you logged onto the cloud you'd be able to see everything that has been sent.'

'I imagine so.' She stands up, walks over to the small computer desk in front of the window, and logs on to her laptop. 'Shit, it's sending a code to my other devices so I can log on to the cloud.' She grabs her iPad, placed next to the laptop, and taps the code sent into her laptop. 'I'm in, but if Leyla has taken my phone, she'll know I've accessed the messages now. The code would have been sent to my phone too.'

'Let's not worry about that. If we can see what messages she's sent to Tom, then we'll know where she's meeting him.'

'Oh my God.' Skye's mouth is open as she stares at the laptop screen in front of her.

'What is it?' I rush over to look at the pictures that she's loaded onto the screen. There's a picture of Tom and Skye sitting across the table from each other in a pub. His hand holding hers, the other holding her chin as he looks into her eyes.

'It's when I met him that time.' I was just going to pop round to your house, but Leyla said I should meet him somewhere in public in case he got aggressive. I had no idea she took a photo of us. Why would she do that? And that photo is so not how it looks. He was trying to persuade me how much he loved you. Look, there's one of us too.' She points to a photograph taken the afternoon when we had the picnic. 'She must have followed me and taken that with her own phone, but for some reason it's been uploaded onto the cloud.'

I recall Tom's strange phone call: *You know as well as I do the photos don't give an accurate picture.* 'She must have sent it to him at some point from your phone, that's why it's been stored on the cloud,' I say. 'What about text messages sent to Tom? Is there anywhere to suggest where they might be meeting? The text I had says *same place* so they must have met somewhere before.'

Skye clicks on the icon and scrolls through messages sent over the last few days. I recognise Tom's mobile number. She's sent him another picture of our daughter with Skye. The caption reads *love child of local councillor torn from mother's arms.*

What about deleted messages? I point to the *deleted* tab.

There's a message dated six weeks ago, just before I'd heard Tom speaking on the phone. *If you don't want your wife finding out what you've been up to then tell her you've changed your mind about the baby.* Attached is the picture of Tom and Skye in the pub.

He replies. *What the hell are you playing at? You know that's not how it looks.*

Another text follows shortly. *Don't contact me on this number again or u can explain 2 ur wife Councillor Smyth. Will contact you when I'm ready.*

A week later there's another text and another picture. It's the one of me and Skye going over her latest assignment as we're having our picnic. She's making notes on her iPad as I point at an open textbook. *How cosy. Does uni know ur wife gives private tuition? I need more money. Leave £500 here...* there's an arrow drawn onto the photo, pointing at a bin next to where we're sitting.

Skye gasps. 'She said she won that £500 on a scratch-card.'

There are no more texts until the day of the birth. The one we both received threatening for more money. And another one sent to Tom. *Oops sent that one to wifey. Soz. We don't want her finding out about our arrangement and getting stressed – not with her health problems... do we? I wonder if she'd like some pics to go with it?*

'I can't believe she'd do this. I just don't understand. Unless... Skye opens the desk drawer and rifles around. 'It's gone. I think I know where she's meeting him.'

'What's gone?' my sister asks.

'Her passport.' She reads out the text Leyla sent to Tom just before he left home: *u have 1 hour or we're leaving without u. Leave money same place as last time.*

The money seems inconsequential. The only words I can focus on are *we're leaving without you.*

My daughter lets out a small cry as she lies in her crib, as if she's urging me to let her father know she's safe. That she's with me. I try his number. Maybe he didn't answer last time because it was my sister ringing. It rings a few times before he answers; he sounds out of breath.

'Kate,' he says. 'It's okay. Everything's sorted. I'm on my way back now.' He sounds weird like he's been to the dentist. 'Can you make your way over to the surrogate's apartment? I'll explain when I get there.'

'I'm already here,' I tell him.

'What? How come?'

'Never mind that. It sounds like we both have some explaining to do. Did you hand over the money?' I ask.

'Yes, and no. I'm just pulling into the street now.' The line goes dead.

As soon as he walks through the door I notice his lip is swollen. There are also splatters of blood on his shirt. With our daughter in my arms, I rush towards him. I reach towards his face but stop a whisper away from touching him.

'What happened?' I ask. 'Surely Leyla didn't do this?' Although I'm starting to realise she's capable of more than I've given her credit for.

'You've worked out she was the one behind it all, then?' Tom says. It's the first time he's seen our daughter and all the time he's talking to me, he can't take his eyes off her.

'Eventually. But we still can't make sense of it all. Would you like to hold our daughter?'

'I think I'd better take this off first. It's okay it's not my blood.' He unbuttons his shirt, so he's just wearing the T-shirt he has on underneath. He walks over to the sofa and sits down, and I hand our baby to him. I can't help but smile as I notice how much she looks like him.

'We know it all started because she wanted to keep our daughter,' I say. 'But apart from the obvious reasons why anybody would need money, we can't understand why she would do what she did. And how she possibly thought she could get away with it.'

'I'm not sure how much you know about what Leyla has been up to.' Tom looks at Skye. 'I'm sorry if what I'm about to say comes as a shock to you. You might want to sit down.'

'No, it's okay. To be honest, after everything I've learned about her today, I've come to realise she's not the person I thought she was.'

'It was after I picked you up from work last night, that it all began to fit together,' he says to me.

'Do you remember, she walked past and spoke to you as you got in the car?'

'Yes, I remember.' It's hard to believe that this time yesterday, I thought she was just another ordinary colleague. 'You asked who she was, that you recognised her from somewhere, and I said she was at the Christmas ball the year before last and was sitting at our table.'

'But that's not the only place I recognised her from. I'm sorry if I kept a few things from you, darling, but it was only to protect you. You know how you need to avoid stressful situations as much as possible.'

'Go on.'

'A few months ago, Skye contacted me. She'd heard rumours I was having an affair and was worried about our daughter being raised in an unstable environment.' Our daughter stirs. Tom gently rocks her in his arms, and she drifts back to sleep. 'It was totally unfounded; complete nonsense.' Tom looks at me intensely, urging me to believe him.

'It's okay. I know about it.'

'You do?'

'I've only just found out.'

'Well, there was this girl with her, who was introduced to me as Leyla. Her bright-red hair made her stand out, and I thought I recognised her from somewhere. If you remember, when we met at the Christmas ball, she had her hair tied up, it didn't seem quite such a vivid colour then; so although I knew somewhere in the back of my mind that I'd seen her before, I couldn't quite place where. I thought little of it until I started receiving threats with photos of me and Skye; which had been taken when we met at the pub. The threats came from Skye's phone, but it was obvious somebody else was involved; the person who'd taken the photo. I remembered Leyla had gone to the bar, and from the angle of the photo, that's from where it must have been taken. Then when we saw her last night, and you said she worked in the admin office at the uni, I realised that must be how Skye knew things we hadn't told her. About your inherited heart condition that she'd threatened me with in a text. That sort of thing would be on your HR records. I also remembered what you'd said about bumping into her at the hospital, and then later that she'd lost her baby but her girlfriend was pregnant. I hadn't realised they were a couple when I met them in the pub.'

'It's all making sense now,' I say. 'But how did you get the bruised lip, and where did the blood come from?'

'After collecting the money from your sister last night, I drove here and parked up down the road. As you know, we were told to wait for further instructions but that seemed ridiculous. We knew who was blackmailing us. I just wanted to get it over, to get our daughter out of there. I was just about to get out of the car when I saw Leyla come out of the apartment. I watched as she walked down the road, then I followed her. A man was waiting for her just around the corner. He kissed her but she seemed nervous, looking around to check nobody had seen them. Up until that point, I thought it was our surrogate who was the instigator and her girlfriend was her accomplice, but this changed things. It appeared Leyla had secrets of her own. I didn't know what to do for the best, so I contacted DI Gordon.'

'I thought we decided to keep the police out of this,' I say, annoyed that my husband made such a big decision without discussing it with me first. 'It was too risky.'

'I know, I'm sorry for going behind your back but we were out of our depth; it just felt like I had to do something. There was a spate of blackmail threats on local councillors last year. DI Gordon came into the council offices and gave a talk on how to deal with it. I still had his card in my wallet, so I contacted him. We knew the drop off was to be arranged for today, so he told me to wait. That I should make the drop-off as planned and he and one of his colleagues would be watching.'

'What did this man look like?' Skye asks.

'He must have been late twenties/early thirties, short dark hair. He was stocky, a couple of inches shorter than me. Do you recognise him?'

'It sounds like Kaleb, her ex. Leyla is bi. She left him because he was such a loser. Not only did he constantly cheat on her, but he was physically violent too. I can't believe she's gone back to him.'

'So, he was the one behind it all?' my sister asks.

'It seems that way, although Leyla is far from innocent. He might have come up with the idea, but she played a big part in it all. And it seems she was set on double-crossing him too.'

'She's crazy.' Skye brings her hand up to her mouth and gasps. 'Kaleb's a total psycho. She managed to escape him once. She was struck off as a nurse because of him. What the hell is she thinking of getting involved with him again like that. What do you mean by double-crossing him?'

'After I left the money in the bin, I stood under one of the trees. It was far enough not for Leyla to recognise me from that distance, but it gave me a view of the bin. Besides, DI Gordon was posing as an assistant in the tea shop, wiping down the outside tables, and his female colleague was pretending to be a customer, nursing a cup of tea.'

'I know where you mean,' Skye interrupted. 'There's usually a few dog walkers and joggers in that part of the park, so you would have blended in with them.'

'That's what I thought.' Tom nodded. 'Anyway, Leyla picked up the bag as expected. DI Gordon's colleague followed her, but as she walked away the same man I'd seen her with the night before – this Kaleb person - ran up and tried to snatch the bag from her.'

'That must be why her passport is missing, if she was intending to escape with Kaleb's cut of the money,' Skye looks at me, then my sister.

'There was a struggle. DI Gordon's female colleague wrestled him to the floor. Leyla managed to keep hold of the bag and ran off, but DI Gordon chased after her. This female detective almost had Kaleb cuffed, but he managed to free himself and was soon back on his feet and chasing after Leyla.

'That sounds like him.' Skye says. 'Slimy toad.'

'What either of them didn't realise was that they were running towards me. The look on her face when she saw me was a picture. She was so taken aback she froze, not knowing which way to turn. I took advantage of the situation and got the bag off her, but this ex of hers soon caught up. It was obvious he was used to violence, hence the swollen lip, but he was no match for a boisterous Labrador who was having his daily exercise in the park.'

'Oh my goodness,' my sister says. 'Did the dog bite his leg?'

'Not his leg, no,' Tom explains. 'When I was watching from under the tree, I could see the owner throwing the ball, and the Labrador would soon find it and come running back to his owner with the ball in its mouth. The man, who was hobbling about with a walking stick, looked worn out. You know how hot it's been today, and he made me feel even hotter just looking at him, in his cream blazer and straw boater hat; but he kept throwing the ball for his dog until it went into the bushes and the dog couldn't find it. That was when Kaleb tried to get the bag from me. He punched me in the face and wrestled me to the floor.'

'Oh, Tom,' I say, shocked that things could have turned out much worse.

'He was on top of me, his backside in the air when the Labrador came bounding up, thinking it was some kind of game. Let's just say although the dog lost one ball, he found another. It looks like Kaleb will be in hospital for a while yet.'

Jodi

Mine

The full moon filtered through the small dusty window as sticky crimson blood pooled around my feet. My heart was racing, yet I could hardly breathe. The fear of losing my unborn baby gripped me as if it were happening for real.

A midwife appeared from nowhere. 'It's okay, poppet, have this one instead.' She handed me a newborn baby that quickly morphed into a fully grown toddler.

I knew I was dreaming, but illogical thought told me I had to save the baby thrust into my care. I needed to wake up; escape to a place of safety. But I couldn't.

The familiar sound of my alarm trilled out, rescuing me from the night and bringing me back into my real daytime world as I woke covered in sweat.

The recurring nightmare had invaded my sleep for several days in a row now. So all-consuming, it haunted my waking hours, leaving me unsure of whether it was a nightmare or if it had happened for real. I reached out and silenced the alarm on my iPhone, whilst making sure it stayed within grabbing distance. Ben had already left for work and I needed to know he was there at the other end of the phone should I need him.

Scared of the ghostly emptiness waiting downstairs, I didn't want to leave the safety of my bed, but the sound of my eighteen-month-old daughter's cry pierced the eerie silence, and my maternal instinct kicked in, forcing my fears aside. I rushed to the nursery, grabbing my dressing gown, and placing my phone in the pocket, like a protective suit of armour that would save me from anything evil lurking in the shadows.

'Shush, it's okay, Patsy, baby,' I whispered in my daughter's tiny ear as I lifted her out of her cot and held her close. 'Mummy's here.' The knot in my stomach loosened as I drew comfort from her sweet baby breath caressing my neck.

Autonomy of my daily routine took over and the fear that gripped me during the night subsided. Downstairs, with Patsy sat in her highchair thirstily drinking her warm milk, I poured myself a coffee whilst simultaneously making scrambled eggs and toasted soldiers. It didn't seem five minutes ago my baby daughter was suckling at my breast every three hours before dropping off to sleep. I remembered the dilemma of risking waking her, so I could lay her down in her crib; or stay exactly as we were, revelling in the delicious moments of post-feed bliss. Now, her newfound craving for scrambled eggs, a sign she was beginning to make her own decisions. No longer an extension of myself, but a little person in her own right.

Unlike the damp darkness of my nightmare, the fresh autumn morning proudly showed off its clear blue sky, enticing people out of their homes. After breakfast, I wrapped Patsy up warmly and ventured outdoors to the park.

'Cat!' Patsy pointed excitedly as she sat in her pushchair whilst I locked the front door.

My new neighbour from across the road appeared out of nowhere, making me jump. 'There you are, Jingles,' she scolded, scooping up her cat who was skulking under the tree outside our house; the protective twigs providing a haven to the family of birds, whose nest was perched up high. 'You're lucky to have such a beautiful child,' she told me like

I didn't know. 'Isn't she beautiful, Jingles?'

'Meow.' Jingles was more interested in the birds' nest and clawed at his owner's arm, making it bleed before escaping her clutches.

Most of our neighbours were too busy to spare anything more than a quick *hello* but Jingles' owner had recently moved into the rented house across the road. She was about the same age as myself; a little younger perhaps, in her late twenties I would say.

'I'm Leyla. You're Jodi, aren't you?' She spoke in the way a child addresses a new classmate.

'Yes,' I told her, curious as to how she knew my name. There was something strangely familiar about her I couldn't quite put my finger on.

Leyla wore denim jeans with a smart aqua-coloured blouse. Unlike my casual mummy up-do, her red hair was ironed to perfection. Her perfume I couldn't quite make out... *Chanel No 5*? I'd never been much of a fan, preferring the light flowery scent of Jimmy Choo's *Blossom*, but there was something else - a strange stale smell that overpowered her expensive perfume.

'Are you okay? Would you like me to clean that up for you?' I asked, pointing to her bleeding arm.

'No. I used to be a nurse. I can do it.' She covered the bleeding scratch with the hand of her other arm. 'I have to go now. Chloe will be home soon.' Then she was gone. Jingles at her heels, leaving me wondering who Chloe might be.

Back at home that evening, with Patsy settled for the night, I snuggled up on the sofa in front of the TV with Ben. We opened a bottle of sauvignon. It had been an exhausting day. Patsy loved running around the park; she couldn't sit still for five minutes that one. I'd taken lots more photos and posted them on Facebook. It was the best way to share them with my family who lived in Australia.

'We're so lucky to have such a healthy little girl.' Ben said, pulling me in closer as he kissed me on the top of my head. We were watching an episode of Holby City where a young baby was undergoing life-saving heart surgery.

'I know. There isn't a day goes by that I don't count our blessings.' I shuddered as I thought about how things might have been. When she was born, the doctors said Patsy had a heart defect, but when she underwent further tests it had disappeared. Just like that.

We finished the bottle of wine, then opened another. I was starting to nod off.

'Come on, sleepyhead. It's time for bed.' Ben

stood up and switched off the TV.

Upstairs in bed, afraid of the hell that awaited me on the other side of sleep, I tried to keep my eyes open; but exhaustion overpowered me. There was no bright moon this time. I was in complete darkness except for a pair of bright blue eyes, just like Ben's, staring out from the inky-black space. A child's haunting voice called *Mama, save me, Mama,* as an arm grabbed me and I woke up. Or did I?

It was the weekend and Ben was home, so we went for a stroll along the seafront. Ben pushed Patsy's stroller as I walked by his side, when I noticed Leyla with a man.

'Hi, this is Ben,' Leyla told us proudly.

'Another Ben. How fabulous,' I said. 'Don't you think he looks just like you, darling?' I turned to look at my husband. But he wasn't there. Neither was Patsy. When I looked back at Leyla and her boyfriend, they'd gained a baby in a pushchair. A baby that looked just like Patsy.

'Mama,' Patsy said.

'Hello, sweetheart.' I bent down so I could speak to Patsy at eye level.

'No, my mama. Not you!' Patsy hit me in the face. She was straining in her seat. The straps digging into her. She no longer spoke like an eighteen-month-old but a child around four years of age.

Monday morning arrived. Ben was at work, and I decided to pay Leyla a visit. My dream had been so real, I was no longer certain where my dreams ended and real life began. I needed to find out if she had a boyfriend called Ben. Maybe it was just an example of the events of the day influencing the things you dreamed about, but to be honest that was what worried me the most.

I walked out of my garden gate and turned left.

'Me go swings.' Patsy had started to string a few words together over the last week.

'Later, sweetheart. We're just going to see Leyla first.'

Patsy had no idea who Leyla was, of course, but I often spoke to my daughter as if she understood everything. A much better alternative to speaking to myself.

The houses on Leyla's side of the road were bigger than mine, with two reception rooms and a cellar. Leaving the pushchair at the bottom of the four steep steps leading to Leyla's front door, I rang the doorbell. She answered straight away. If I didn't know any better, I would have said she was expecting me.

'How wonderful to see you again.' Placing her door on the latch, she made her way down the steps and lifted Patsy out of her stroller before taking her inside. 'I knew you'd come back, Chloe.'

I was about to tell her my name wasn't Chloe but realised she was talking to Patsy, not me. 'My daughter's name is Patsy, not Chloe,' I said, following her into the hallway. The house had the same strange odour that I'd smelled on Leyla when she first spoke to me.

Leyla turned to face me, hitching Patsy higher onto her hip and pulling her in tighter to her breast. 'I'm afraid you must leave now, it's time for Chloe's nap.'

Coming here was a mistake. I needed to get Patsy away from her but was afraid things could go wrong if I made the wrong move. It felt like I'd returned to my nightmare. I knew I hadn't, but it was as if they were connected somehow. Subconscious thoughts leaking into my dreams. Who was this unhinged woman, and how did I know her? There was a hint of recognition, but it was trapped in the corners of my mind, just out of reach.

'You know I can't do that, Leyla. You need to give Patsy back to me, now.' I tried to remain calm. To reassure Patsy that everything was okay. She didn't like being held for too long even by me or Ben, let alone a stranger.

'Chloe is mine. You can't have her anymore.' Leyla was making gentle rocking movements; backwards and forwards, side to side. Patsy was fidgeting, but at least Leyla was trying to pacify her.

'Leyla, I don't know who Chloe is, but you're holding my daughter, Patsy.'

'No, your daughter's dead. See for yourself if you don't believe me.' Leyla's house had a completely different layout to mine. There was a door leading from the hallway to the cellar. She kicked it open. But there was no way I was going down there.

Leyla was a good five inches taller than I was. Her toned arms no doubt much stronger than mine. I scanned my surroundings for something I could use as a weapon. There was a golfing umbrella propped up against the wall but it was closer to Leyla. I couldn't risk it. I noticed a photograph on the side table. A woman and a newborn baby. The corners of my mind were loosening. I recalled the shy girl with red bobbed hair that I'd shared a room with at the hospital when I had Patsy. On the surface, she was barely recognisable as that person, but it was definitely her. Her voice and the small scar just below her right eye. The Facebook friend request I'd received a few weeks ago. Her profile picture was of her cat. She'd sent me a private message. *Where are you living now? We should meet up.* I had every intention of replying; but then the nightmares started. With little sleep, I was too exhausted to think about getting in touch with somebody I barely knew.

Patsy struggled. 'Park now, Mama,' she said, holding out her arms to me.

I attempted to grab her, but Leyla pulled her back.

'Leyla, please. You're upsetting my daughter. Just give her back to me.'

'No. I told you, she's mine. I switched the name tags at the hospital. As an ex-nurse, it was easy for me to swap babies and fit a new ID tag.'

I remembered how our babies looked so similar. The nurses were always so busy rushing around. Leyla and I would take turns to look after each other's baby whilst we had a shower. A midwife had remarked how you could only tell them apart by their hats and joked about not getting them mixed up.

'Why on earth would you do that?'

'Kaleb, my ex, was demanding custody. I lied and told him Chloe wasn't his, but he was insisting on a DNA test. I only meant it to be a temporary swap until I proved he wasn't the father.'

I recalled him coming in, shouting at Leyla. Telling her she was an unfit mother. I remembered security throwing him out and thinking about what might happen if he came back when Leyla was looking after Patsy.

'Then you told me the doctors thought your baby had a heart defect, but a second test showed it had been a mistake. Except it wasn't. I had the sick baby. You had mine. I was going to switch them back, but you never let her out of your sight again.'

I felt sick as I realised how, in trying to protect my daughter, I'd placed her in danger. After the scene with Leyla's ex, I'd waited until Ben came in to visit before having my daily shower. I didn't want that man coming anywhere near my baby.

'I moved here especially to put things back the way they were. But now your baby is dead. This is Chloe, not Patsy, and she's mine.'

The cellar door opened a little wider as Jingles appeared to investigate his visitors. The strange malodorous odour lingering in the hall hit me in the face. Vomit threatened to escape my throat.

Patsy spotted Jingles and was struggling for Leyla to put her down. Leyla yanked her up higher onto her hip in an attempt to restrain her, but hadn't bargained on how much of a fondness Patsy had for cats. Patsy lashed out, kicking and screaming.

'Get outside, Jingles.' Leyla had taken her eyes off me for a split second. Her attention divided between wanting me to leave and trying to stop her cat, who was rubbing against her leg, vying for attention.

I attempted to grab Patsy, but Leyla pulled her back.

Patsy struggled even more; inadvertently head-butting Leyla in the nose. 'Park now, Mama,' she said, holding out her arms to me.

With Leyla temporarily stunned, I took advantage and snatched my daughter away from her. If what Leyla said was true, and Patsy wasn't my biological daughter, the intensity of her little arms clinging around my neck told me none of that mattered; the bond we had could never be broken.

Leyla tried to take her from me. 'Oh no, you don't bitch,' I yelled, pulling backwards. My maternal strength overpowering even Leyla's psychotic force.

The excitement was too much for Jingles who was circling his owner's feet, ignoring her instructions to get outside. As Leyla lost her grip on Patsy, the force of her own strength sent her stumbling backwards into Jingles who darted for his life into the cellar. I took advantage whilst Leyla was off balance and gave her a helping hand to join Jingles. Leyla screamed, and I heard a thud. Fearful she would come after me, I panicked and locked both Leyla and her cat in the cellar.

Was Leyla telling the truth? Was my biological daughter dead? Was she in the cellar? I had to find out for myself, but first I needed to make sure Patsy was safe. I made my way outside, grateful I'd left the stroller at the bottom of the steps. Patsy was reluctant to let go of me, but I knew I'd reach the safety of home much quicker if I didn't have to carry her. I grabbed the stroller in one hand and dragged it out into the street before strapping Patsy into the seat.

The street where I live, or avenue to be precise with its scattering of oak trees growing outside every other cluster of semi-detached houses, is a shortcut to the retail park. The popularity of the new bargain-basement store coming at the expense of the once quiet residential area, now being a rat-run.

I didn't see the car until it was too late. I thrust Patsy's stroller forward out of harm's way before pain shot through me like nothing I'd felt before. Then everything went black.

***

Once again, I'm wrapped in darkness. There's a drug-infused stench hanging in the air, but this time it's different. I can hear Ben's voice and feel the touch of his tender hand holding mine as he tries to reassure me everything is going to be okay.

'I have to go soon, babe.' I feel the warmth of his breath on my cheek as he kisses me goodbye.

No, don't go. Don't leave me, she'll kill me, I try to tell him, but the words won't come. An eerie beeping noise is coming from the other side of the wall; and voices… familiar, comforting voices.

'Help!' But my pleading goes unnoticed and the bleeping becomes more erratic.

The darkness is lifting. It's foggy but I can just make out that Ben is still here. So are my mother and father, medical staff and… 'Leyla,' I attempt to mutter through my dry lips as I wake from my coma.

'Don't worry about that just now, my love.' I feel the delicate trace of my mother's fingers on my face. 'You need to rest.'

But she doesn't understand. Standing beside my mother is Leyla. Her face bruised and battered, her clothes blood-stained. Her head fallen to one side, unsupported by her broken neck.

~~~

Colin

The Story Collector – Part 4

Colin often played a game with his dog, where he would fake throwing a ball but put it in his pocket. A trick that kept Billie busy whilst he took a little breather. But she would go to any lengths to find it. Colin often found himself in some embarrassing situations, not to mention near misses, where Billie would approach strangers to hunt out her ball in the most inappropriate places. And it was one such occurrence that gave him the idea for Kaleb's unfortunate episode.

With Colin and his wife, Pat, not being blessed with a child of their own, leaving Kaleb sterile was the worst possible fate that Colin could imagine. That should have been the extent of any revenge. However, characters can sometimes take on a life of their own, leaving the author with no say in the matter; and whilst Kaleb was left unable to father any future children, Leyla had already conceived. Her own story was itching to be told. But Colin hadn't planned on any further twists in the tale; and rogue links in the chain of acquaintance, that deviate from the predetermined route, can have devastating consequences for a character.

Listening to Jodi's poem about post-natal depression and how she was unable to bond with her baby daughter, had been an emotional rollercoaster. She'd written a stanza on how she'd been paranoid that her daughter had been swapped by one of the nurses. But the final stanza had left the writing group in tears as Jodi described how once the depression had lifted, the love she felt for her daughter had knocked her sideways. Everybody in the group knew little Patsy and how much joy she brought to Jodi's life. And with Jodi's permission, Colin found a way in to Leyla's story.

But once *Mine* had been published, Colin couldn't stop thinking about the fate of the fictional Jodi's biological daughter. Was she really dead in Leyla's cellar? Or had something else happened to her? It was time for Colin to return to his writing journal and reunite Jodi with Chloe.

In Colin's sequel, it turned out Chloe had been taken into care following a violent incident between Leyla and Kaleb, where Chloe was caught in the crossfire and received a broken arm. The malodorous smell emanating from the cellar was several dead birds that Jingles had brought home for his owner, which Leyla then used to try and entice Jodi into the cellar, in an attempt to kidnap Patsy. A plan that failed miserably.

After coming around from the coma, Jodi's incoherent ramblings of the woman who'd invaded her nightmares whilst she'd been unconscious - including the nightmare where she dreamed of being woken from the coma to see a dead Leyla at the foot of her bed - were believed to be a side effect of the traumatic injuries she received in the accident.

It was several weeks before Leyla was found in the cellar when her mother hadn't heard from her. And nobody made the link between Jodi being knocked down not far from Leyla's house, and Leyla's body being discovered several weeks later.

Jodi didn't report what Leyla told her about Patsy not being her real daughter. She knew Leyla's death was an accident but what if the judge didn't believe her? She couldn't risk going to prison and losing her daughter.

Colin hadn't meant for Kaleb to become embroiled in such a twist, but with his history of violence towards Leyla - including the time when he hit her so hard, she was left with a scar just below her right eye - he was charged with her murder. And although he wasn't guilty of Leyla's murder, if it hadn't been for him then none of it would have happened. So, in a way, it was poetic justice.

Once Jodi learned that Chloe was alive and well, she applied to adopt the daughter of her friend that used to live across the road. Messages that Leyla had sent to Jodi on Facebook proved their friendship went right back to the birth of their daughters, and social services had no problem with Jodi and Ben becoming Chloe's adopted parents.

Colin's last story had flowed. There'd been a force pushing through his fingertips and it was as if the pen his wife had bought for his birthday had become enchanted. But what had spooked Colin was when Rik reported what had happened to the non-fictionalised Kaleb, or Blake in real life.

Colin knew his stories often teetered on the edge of fact and fiction. Lucas and Abby – or Claus and Babs - had seemed just a coincidence. After all, he'd done his utmost to push them together. And when

Tina inherited a house from an old lady who she'd helped when the old lady could no longer look after her dog - whilst bearing a strange similarity to Colin's story, it did not come as a surprise as kindness is often paid back through Karma. But when Blake was sent to prison for the manslaughter of a girl he'd met on Tinder – after pushing her down a staircase, Colin knew there was more to his story collecting abilities than he'd first thought.

The one sad change in Colin's life in recent months had been the death of his beloved dog, Billie. With no children of his own, Billie had turned his house into a home. Colin couldn't have loved her more if she had been human, and the place just wasn't the same without her. Maybe he would open up his heart to another pet in the future, but for the moment, losing her was too raw. In an attempt to fill the gaping hole in his heart, Colin wrote more and more stories, but the one genre he couldn't seem to master was the fairy tale. Until one day, whilst out for a walk, he noticed an advertisement on the door of the local community centre.

Do you like a good story?
Have you ever wanted to master

the art of creative writing?
Come and join us on Wednesday evenings.
Learn about the great Russian folklorist,
Vladimir Propp.
Who knows – perhaps you could
write your own fairy tale?

Colin had heard Abby speak of Vladimir Propp. She'd done well in her literature degree with the Open University, and had told him some fascinating things about literature that he hadn't heard of. One of them was how this twentieth-century folklorist identified the types of character and structural elements of fairy tales. Maybe this was just what Colin needed; learning a new skill might occupy his mind and help him get over losing Billie.

Another person that Colin couldn't put out of his mind was Mary. She'd been a good neighbour to Abby, and Colin was shocked to learn Mary wasn't a widow at all. Her husband had gone missing after an afternoon at his allotment, and it was quite a mystery what had happened to him. But that was all about to change, as Colin settled into his usual Wednesday evening seat in the make-shift classroom at the community centre, and put his pen to paper to write his first fairy-tale…

Jemma and Mary

The Pump-King

It was exactly one year since Jemma's grandfather had disappeared. There one minute and gone the next. Jemma had tried her best to keep the allotment going, but Grandma had now given up hope of Grandfather ever returning and had grown a few of her favourite vegetables in her small garden instead.

'I need you to collect Grandfather's wheelbarrow from the allotment,' Grandma said to Jemma as she rubbed cubes of butter into a bowl of flour. Oscar, her cocker spaniel, sat patiently waiting for any scraps of food to fall to the floor. 'The rent is paid until the end of the month, after that I will have to let it go.'

'Of course, Grandma.' Jemma had been

dreading this moment but knew it was inevitable. Sadness ripped through her as she remembered how Grandfather had shown her how to grow vegetables from a tiny seed, the calming feeling of the cool soil between her fingers providing tranquillity in an otherwise stressful world. 'I was just about to take Oscar for a walk so I'll pick up the barrow whilst I'm out.'

'You're a good girl. In return, I shall make your favourite pumpkin pie for tea. The garden may be small, but its south-facing position and rich soil have produced a good crop this year. Grandfather would be proud.'

At the allotment, Jemma stepped into the shed. She thought back to the day Grandfather disappeared: the teabag left brewing in a mug of boiling water as if his morning cuppa was expecting him to return. And Halloween of all days. The allotment committee's Pump-King Competition had always been a special occasion, and last year Grandfather's prize pumpkin was bigger than ever. *No,* Jemma thought, there was no way Grandfather would just walk away from everything, not by choice. But what other explanation was there?

'Sorry to disturb you, but could you give me a

hand?' It was the neighbour on the adjacent allotment plot.

'Yeah, sure.' Jemma followed the neighbour to find a huge pumpkin growing from the ground.

'If you could lift that side, then I can do this side.' The neighbour might have been an old man, but Jemma couldn't help admire the size and strength of his hands and arms as he lifted the pumpkin.

'Oscar, move boy. You'll get squished if that thing falls on you.' But Oscar kept sniffing and scratching at the base of the pumpkin, and when it was lifted from the ground his scratching became more erratic as he barked excitedly.

'Thanks for your help,' the neighbour said as they placed the pumpkin into his wheelbarrow. He really was quite peculiar looking. His brown neckbeard emphasised his long yet stubby nose, and those huge hairy hands and forearms were quite at odds with his short and skinny legs.

'I'll just put it in your shed for you.' Jemma lifted the handle of the barrow and walked over to the neighbour's shed.

'No,' the neighbour said abruptly. Then more calmly, 'It's okay, I'll do it.'

'It's no trouble.' Jemma stepped closer to the shed door and pushed it open.

'I said I'll do it.'

'Okay; whatever. Come on, Oscar. Oscar boy, where have you got to now?' Jemma looked around just in time to catch a glimpse of Oscar's wagging tail before it disappeared into the hole left by the pumpkin. She ran over, but the hole was closing. Jemma frantically scooped away the soil with her hands, then suddenly her whole body was sucked forward as if the soil was quicksand. 'Help,' she called. But the neighbour had already disappeared into his shed.

WHOOOSH! Jemma somersaulted through the tunnel before landing on a muddy floor. There were candles spaced out along the walls, leading to what looked like a wider cave. Jemma gingerly stood up, rubbing her buttocks, which had taken the brunt of the fall. Oscar came scampering towards her before running away again to explore the strange surroundings. She could hear noises coming from deeper in the cave, digging and voices. She made her way forward slowly. It was much lighter here, vegetables were growing everywhere and over by the pumpkin section she saw Oscar being fussed over by a familiar face.

'Grandfather!' Jemma ran towards him, not

quite believing her eyes.

'Hello, my love.' Grandfather hugged Jemma just like he did when she was a young girl. 'It's great to see you. Just look how much you've grown. And Grandmother – how is she?'

'Grandma's okay. She misses you, of course. But what are you doing here? Did you get here the same way as I did?'

'No. I came through the portal in Master Mole's shed.' Grandfather looked around to check if anybody was watching. 'You must have come through the old tunnel. It's directly below Master Mole's pumpkin plot. His greed for growing the biggest pumpkin, together with Oscar's digging must have weakened it.'

'Good old Oscar. He knew where to find you. Grandma is going to be made up.'

'I'm sorry Jemma, my love, I can't leave. And you can't stay. This needs to be our secret until...'

'Until what? Why can't you leave? You have to.' This wasn't what Jemma was expecting at all. The only thing she could think about was how they were going to get out of there, but Grandfather seemed happy where he was and just wanted Jemma to leave without him.

'Sorry to disturb you, Grandfather, sir.' A mole-like dwarf approached, bowing as he addressed him. 'Master Mole needs to speak to you in his office. And nice to meet you, miss.' He turned to face Jemma as he bowed again before shuffling off back in the direction he'd come.

Jemma couldn't believe what she was seeing. 'Who's that?'

'That's one of the molemen. They're the workers that keep Vegland going.'

'Vegland?'

'Yes. We supply vegetables for Master Mole's allotment.'

'But that's ridiculous? And who is this Master Mole?'

'It's not up to us to question things. We just get on with it.'

Jemma and Grandfather were interrupted by a bang then a loud scream.

'I'm sorry, I have to go. That poor fellow will be in trouble if I don't hurry and get to Master Mole's office.'

Soon after Grandfather left, the moleman reappeared, holding his pudgy hands to his head.

'Are you okay?' Jemma asked. 'What was that noise?'

'That was Master Mole throwing a pumpkin at

my head. He does that when he's angry.'

'He can't do that. How dare he pick on a little fellow like you? I'm going to have a word with him, see how he likes it.'

'Well, that's kind of you, but please don't. You didn't come through the normal portal; he mustn't know you're here.'

'Normal portal?' It seemed such an oxymoron.

'Master Mole's office. Or his allotment shed, as it is on the other side. The temporary portal in the tunnel you came through, is closed over now.'

'So how do I get to this normal portal, then?' Jemma made quote marks with her fingers as she spoke the word *normal*.

'Oh, dear. You don't know, do you? Every one of us was human once, brought here like Grandfather when Master Mole was in danger of losing the Pump-King Competition against one of us. If you cross Master Mole or if he finds out you've tried to escape, you become a moleman. Grandfather has learned from the mistakes of the rest of us. He knows to bide his time and to trick Master Mole into gaining his trust. That's why he's still in his human form.'

'So, we're stuck here forever?' Jemma scooped up Oscar and held him close.

'There's just one way,' the moleman whispered.

'My life is in danger if I tell you, but nobody's been prepared to stick up for me before.' The moleman held on to Jemma's forearm and pulled her over to the corner of the cave. 'This year's competition is the most important of all. Curse of the moleman was put on Master Mole by a wizard who lost the Pump-king Competition fifty years ago. If Master Mole wins again this year, he is released from the curse and can leave. But if he loses then he dies.'

'And if he wins, what happens to us?'

'The portal closes, and we're trapped forever. But you still have a chance, you and Oscar. You arrived by accident; as long as he doesn't know you're here, you can't be cursed. You need to hide until he leaves for the competition, then you can escape.'

'What about Grandad?'

'Master Mole knows he's here; he can't escape without being turned into a moleman. Once Master Mole wins, Grandfather will be trapped here forever.'

'And if Master Mole doesn't win?'

'The curse is broken. We're all free and the molemen go back to their human form. But that won't happen. Only members of the allotment committee can enter the competition and there are no bigger pumpkins on the allotment. Master Mole has made sure of that.'

'Not on the allotment, no. But you just have to be a committee member to enter; the pumpkin doesn't need to be grown on the allotment. Show me the way to Master Mole's office. I must get out of here. Now.'

'No, wait.' The moleman walked over to one of the pumpkins and lifted off the top. 'Take this,' he said, as he covered his snout with his pudgy paws and held the lethal weapon at arm's length.

'Grandfather's pipe? But why?'

'Master Mole is becoming more mole-like by the hour. Moles hate the smell of tobacco. You're going to have to be devious if you're going to outsmart him. Follow me – but keep that thing away from me.' The moleman pinched his nose with the fingers of one hand and held the palm of his other hand up to the pipe.

Hiding in the alcove next to Master Mole's office, the small moleman handed Jemma a box of matches. 'I need to go now. Wait here until Grandfather leaves before you attempt to light the pipe and go in. If Grandfather sees you, he won't let you risk anything and will stop you.'

It seemed ages before Grandfather reappeared,

but Jemma was careful to follow the instructions given to her.

'Enter,' was the last word Master Mole spoke before the smoke emanating from Grandfather's pipe knocked him out.

With Oscar at her heels, Jemma escaped through the portal, running as fast as she could across the allotment plot towards Grandfather's shed. Doing as Grandma had asked, she grabbed Grandfather's wheelbarrow and ran back to Grandma's house, arriving just as Grandma was about to stick her sharpest kitchen knife into her prize pumpkin

'No. Stop!' Jemma screamed, stopping Grandma in her tracks.

'But I'm just about to make the pumpkin pie.'

'That's gonna have to wait.' Jemma ran into the kitchen and gently lifted Grandma into the wheelbarrow.

'What are you doing?'

'There's no time to explain now. You just need to trust me,' she said, before putting the prize pumpkin onto Grandma's lap and running all the way to the village hall.

They arrived just behind Master Mole, who by now had come around from his unexpected afternoon snooze. Jemma watched as Master Mole arranged his pumpkin on the table, admiring how much bigger it was than all the others.

'There's just one more entry,' the chair of the allotment committee announced as Jemma placed Grandma's prize pumpkin next to Master Mole's. 'And there's no question of doubt this is the winner,' he said, placing a red ribbon adorned with a golden pumpkin-shaped medal around Grandma's neck.

There was a scream from the lady on the cake stall as Master Mole fell to the ground, clutching his chest. 'Call an ambulance,' somebody called, but it was too late. Master Mole was already dead.

'Well done, Grandma,' Jemma said, as she kissed her on the cheek.

'Yes, well done, my love,' a familiar voice said. 'It's good to be back.'

~~~

Our Golden Girl

As golden as the daffodil
The smallest of the bunch;
Unlike your bouncing brothers
You didn't fight or punch.
After watching from a distance
Your turn came for fuss;
But we knew straight away
You were the one for us.

As golden as the velvet sand
No holiday kennels for you;
As part of our family
To the seaside, you came too.
Lapping up the ocean's waves
You were in your element;
Exhausted by the end of day,
Carefree - happy and content.

Our Golden Girl

As golden as the autumn leaves
The park you loved so much;
Running with your canine friends
Playing ball, chase, and touch.
Blustery days never put you off
You made sure we kept fit;
You dragged us up and out each day
Made sure we didn't mope and sit.

As golden as the glowing fire
Your favourite place to be;
Sleeping snuggled on your rug
Beside the Christmas tree.
The snow fell gently on the pane
Enticing you out to play;
But the snowy ocean once a field
Is far too cold today.

The seasons come and go each year;
End of our time with you, too near.
Our darling girl you are so brave
If only love was free to save.
But in our arms you close your eyes,
And now you watch us from the skies.
Our love for you will never part;
Like the gaping hole within our hearts.

~~~

THE STORY COLLECTOR

Acknowledgements

Not only did I write many of these stories as part of the creative writing element of my English Literature degree, I would not have put this collection together had it not been for the support of my writing friends that I've met through The Open University: Suzanne Cox, Claire O'Connor, and Jennie Taylor. We've named our writing group Blanc Page because when we meet up, we drink too much wine and end up not doing any writing! And my final year of study would not have been the same without the brilliant psychological thriller writer, Lisa Hall, as my partner in crime – oops I mean study buddy…

I developed other stories from assignments completed through the Writers' Bureau. My tutor, best-selling crime writer, Sheila Bugler, provided me with the tools to hone my stories and gave me the confidence to bring them to print.

I can't thank my beta readers enough for giving up their time to read these stories: Ali Bacon, Claire O'Connor, Elizabeth Hill, Helen Blenkinsop, Janet Pickering, Jo Ullah, Ruth O'Neill, Shell Mutimer, and Suzanne Cox. I've been lucky to have received feedback from such brilliant writers, and believe the stories flow much better because of it.

My work as a book blogger has not only allowed an insight into the book industry, but also the privilege of getting to know some fantastic authors. I would especially like to thank Carol Mason, Jane Corry, Jane Shemilt, and Louise Jensen for how much they inspire me.

And last, but by no means least, my much-loved family. My husband, Paul, who always supports me in whatever I do. This collection initially included stories, under his pen name of James Kirby, but as the collection developed, we decided to publish separately. I could write an entire book on how amazing each of our four children are. I won't embarrass them, but I'll just say they make me an extremely proud Mumma! Having said that, if it wasn't for our youngest son, this collection would not be what it is. As a comic writer himself, Louis' literary knowledge is outstanding, and he's given an enormous amount of feedback.

I can't publish my first book without mentioning my little study/writing buddies, Poppy our golden spaniel, and Sammy our golden Labrador. Alongside our first golden Labrador, Billie, you might recognise them in a few of these stories!

About the Author

Callie lives in Bristol with her husband - a writer and engineer; and their youngest son – also a writer. They have four children, five grandchildren, a Labrador, a spaniel, and a sixteen-year-old dalmatian catfish.

After attaining a First-Class BA (Hons) in English Literature at The Open University, and devouring books as a book blogger for several years, Callie decided it was time to take her writing seriously. *The Story Collector* is a selection of some of the pieces of short fiction that she wrote as part of her degree, as well as her time as a student with The Writers' Bureau. She will be writing a domestic thriller as part of her MA in Creative Writing at the University of Bristol.

Callie isn't fussy what she drinks as long as it's fizzy – no doubt a subconscious effect of nostalgia from when she used to save her school dinner money and spend it on cider. These days the fizz is more likely to be Moet or Bollinger, but her husband has been known to trick her by filling a champagne flute with Black Rat cider…

Printed in Great Britain
by Amazon